Business and Professional Communication

Business and Professional Communication

A Practical Guide to Workplace Effectiveness

Kathryn Sue Young

Professor and Chair, Department of Communication and Theatre,
Mansfield University

Howard Paul Travis

Emeritus, Mansfield University

WAVELAND

PRESS, INC.

Long Grove, Illinois

For information about this book, contact:
  Waveland Press, Inc.
  4180 IL Route 83, Suite 101
  Long Grove, IL 60047-9580
  (847) 634-0081
  info@waveland.com
  www.waveland.com

About the Authors

Kathryn Sue Young has taught at the college level for over 25 years at The Pennsylvania State University, Clarion University, University of Central Arkansas, and is currently a full professor and chair of the Department of Communication and Theatre at Mansfield University. She has published *Group Discussion: A Practical Guide to Participation and Leadership*, 4th edition, with Wood, Phillips, and Pedersen, which is also available in Korean. She has also published numerous articles, including an article in a joint American-Russian publication, and has presented numerous papers at national conferences. She is active in the community, sharing her expertise in parliamentary procedure.

Howard Travis taught at the university level for 37 years. His former students work nationally and globally in electronic media as on-air talent, writers, producers, directors, technicians, sales executives, lawyers, public relations/promotion practitioners, media managers, and media CEOs. He retired early from his teaching career in 2002. Mansfield University of Pennsylvania awarded him professor emeritus status, and he holds the rank of Honorary Professor of Communication, Volgograd State University, Volgograd, Russia.

Together they have published three editions of *Oral Communication: Skills, Choices, and Consequences*, as well as *Communicating Nonverbally: A Practical Guide to Presenting Yourself More Effectively*.

Contents

2   Intrapersonal Examination   19

3   Job Searches, Résumés,   39
   and Cover Letters

4   Interviewing   61

5   Basic Skills for the First Week   81

6   Writing Skills and Technology   105
for the First Week and Beyond

Technology and the Workplace   120

Final Thoughts   125

7   Teamwork and Your Career   127

8   Decision Making, Problem Solving, Leadership, and Management   147

9 Presentational Speaking 169

10 Potentially Threatening or Uncomfortable Communication 189

11 Good Things to Know Something About 203

Preface

Did you ever purchase a puzzle to work on for relaxation and entertainment? If so, you understand that it takes time to put it together. The puzzle you select normally catches your eye due to the image presented on the box cover. As you open the box and dump its contents on a flat surface, you begin to notice the size and shapes of its pieces as well as the total number of pieces to assemble for completion of the image. Then you begin the process of turning each piece over to examine where it might fit in the total design, arranging pieces by color so they relate to specific areas within the picture. You quickly realize that putting the entire image together is going to take more time than you originally planned. Some puzzles are quite complex and take days or weeks to complete. They are a great exercise in problem solving.

Solving a puzzle is a great metaphor for the time and effort you need to spend preparing for a career in business and the professions. Just as you choose a puzzle based on the image on the box cover, you need to create an image (brand) that employers recognize as a good fit for their company. Image is rooted in appearance, specific skills, and abilities. The initial skills that attract the attention of employers are your physical appearance, your sense of movement and physical style, and your extemporaneous use of language in a variety of settings. These "pieces" of your personal brand help strangers remember your name and give them a sense of what you will be like as a colleague. Initial skills assist you in getting a job, but it is your hidden skills that will allow you to succeed.

The hidden skills that cement your brand in the minds of colleagues include: excellent writing skills, consistent use of language (verbal and written), problem-solving skills, solid use of technology and social media, enthusiasm for work and people, a moral and ethical foundation, the ability to adapt quickly to new ideas, and being a role model for others. Mastery of these skills and abilities can propel you toward a position as a manager and leader within an organization. These hidden skills are part of your image, but because they take time to reveal themselves, others do not "see" your true image until they work with you over a period of time.

The initial skills and hidden skills of every working person need constant monitoring and improvement. A career spans decades. Therefore, your skill set will be challenged by new technology, changing corporate culture, and a diverse workforce. It is helpful to recognize this complexity as you undertake the process of molding your skills and abilities into a professional image that makes you appealing to others. This book will enhance this process by helping you recognize and strengthen the personal communication skills necessary to present a consistent, professional image throughout your career.

Acknowledgments

This book was a joyful writing experience. Its many concepts became a mirror in which my entire career reflected back to me. Perhaps the best reflection of all was one of a business door opening wide, thus allowing me to join the ranks of the employed. My working life began with a generous person giving me the chance to prove myself. As I walked through my open door, I met Howard Scammon. Mr. Scammon, Chairman of Theatre and Speech at The College of William and Mary, was a true Southern gentleman whose constant smile, gracious use of language, welcoming personality, and insightful mentoring made me see the possibilities of life as a teacher. His constant encouragement and words of wisdom made my time in Williamsburg truly memorable. I trust my academic career reinforced his faith in me because I am not sure what I would have done with my life had it not been for the door he opened. Thank you, Mr. Scammon. *HPT*

I echo Howard's comments. Three of my professors—Arlie Parks, Dennis Gouran, and Gerald M. Phillips—opened doors for me. Dr. Parks showed me the road to graduate school when I was an undergraduate student. I would never have made it there without her guidance. When I was a young, inexperienced graduate student close to Ph.D. completion, Dr. Gouran told me I would present a paper at the National Communication Association convention. I had never flown or done anything of that magnitude, and I was terrified, but he pushed me forward. Dr. Phillips handed me my first job interview in a department where he knew someone. That piece of networking along with the skill and knowledge that I had developed under his mentorship resulted in my first university position. After that I was ready to fly on my own. I will always treasure their willingness to believe in me. *KSY*

Connections in the business world are invaluable and through one we met our publishers, Carol and Neil Rowe at Waveland Press, Inc. Carol and Neil are the most remarkably warm people you could possibly meet. Their constant encouragement throughout the writing process can never be repaid. If we could pick a couple to live next door to us, we would pick them. Our conversations simply flow, and the laughter is not to be believed. What a team! Thanks to them for all they do to make writing such a pleasure. And, many thanks for hiring such a talented staff.

In addition, we must mention several students. Deb Marbaker for some initial research, Jon Fuller and Ty Cyr for the idea of Ethical Encounter boxes, Holly Baker for the résumé and cover letter, Sarah Lohrer and Lacy Stocum for some last-minute editing and good catches, Steve Daily for some real-world examples, Anine Stanley for sharing her mother's concept of a personal representative, and students in the Business and Professional class from the Spring 2009 to Spring 2011 semesters who gave us plenty of ideas and suggestions. All of the ideas were helpful, and the following students gave us specific examples that we were able to use. We thank them deeply: Randi Brauchle, Tracy Jellif, Breann Hass, Matt Lehman, Jill Butters, Cali Golden, Megan Ruby, Meredith Bennett, Marianne Fisne, Matt Gant, and CJ Sweet.

Finally, we would like to express our sincerest gratitude to Laurie Prossnitz from Waveland Press who did last minute editing and survived our last minute changes with grace and humor. We thoroughly enjoyed working with her!

Communicating for Career Success

GOALS

After reading this chapter you should be able to:

✓ Explain the importance of communication

✓ Describe the components of communication

✓ Analyze problems and propose correctives to communication situations

✓ Select the appropriate channel for your communication

✓ Explain how noise influences communication

✓ Explain and practice the four communication situations

✓ Analyze the four realities of communication

You might be one of the fortunate individuals who secures a decent job prior to graduation or shortly thereafter. Or, maybe you are reading this book prior to seeking full-time employment. In that case, you have strategic planning to do before acquiring an initial job interview. It is important to analyze yourself and your career goals as you decide where to apply. Obtaining an interview is only the first hurdle to clear in a competitive marketplace, and securing an interview by no means indicates you will be selected for the job.

A job interview is the most important persuasive speech you'll ever give because it initiates your career. You'll make your employment journey easier when you recognize the value of communication skills, which include perceived warmth, comprehensive verbal ability, appropriate appearance, expansive writing skills, cooperative interpersonal qualities, and technical abilities (transmitting your ideas through electronic message sharing). Potential employers notice these communication skills immediately. Having good interpersonal skills and being able to give memorable answers to questions during an interview places you ahead of other job applicants.

Once you receive and accept an offer, there are a multitude of unknowns that will flash through your mind as you approach your new office space for the first day: Will you enjoy the job? Will you be prepared for the work that is handed to you? Will you be able to personalize your work space? How will you get along interpersonally with your colleagues? How will your use of time affect your success? Will your attire be appropriate and what does it communicate to others? Will you make a good first impression? Good communication skills provide a solid foundation for positive answers to these questions.

Whether you are seeking a job or have been in a position for a while, future advancement in an organization is critical for sustaining a productive, professional career. A typical career is approximately forty years in length. It is important to establish a strong foundation for your career and to build upon this base with solid achievements. Along the way, strong communication skills will be your most valuable tool. Whether you are leading a team project, sending a mass e-mail to clients, or participating in a virtual environment, every communication will help demonstrate that you are a professional communicator and valuable colleague. Remember, promotions and/or careers have been derailed by sloppy, impulsive, inappropriate, or unprofessional communication. The material in the following chapters will help you avoid such pitfalls.

This book blends the theories of intrapersonal communication, interpersonal communication, nonverbal communication, gender communication, public speaking, group communication, organizational communication, and intercultural communication to focus on the essential skills for communicating appropriately in a business setting. Let's begin with a basic review of the communication process to establish the foundation for professional business communication.

COMMUNICATION ESSENTIALS

Communication is an interactive process between individuals where they share meaning verbally and/or nonverbally. The definition of communication is quite simple, but its execution is rather complicated since participants vary in culture, language usage, and career background. You are familiar with verbal messages and their intended meaning, but nonverbal messages—every gesture you make, the clothes you wear, or even just the way you walk around the office—also communicate information to colleagues observing and evaluating you. Personal observation is an ongoing process and the judgments made about you are cumulative.

We categorize communication as intentional or unintentional. For example, can you remember making a remark you never intended for someone else to hear—but they did? While unplanned communication may not have had long-lasting consequences in a junior high school setting, the consequences of unintentional communication in a business setting can be devastating. Everyone who hears a word or phrase of unintentional or thoughtless communication remembers it. Your verbal carelessness could haunt you in the future.

It is important to understand that your goal in communicating is to share meaning effectively. Communication occurs whether others interpret it correctly or incorrectly. When someone interprets the meaning of language incorrectly, we call it miscommunication, but it remains communication nevertheless. If you become known as someone who can't exchange ideas clearly in a professional setting, you are establishing a pattern of unprofessional behavior that may lead to eventual career failure.

To communicate effectively in business, you must first understand:

- The importance of appropriate communication
- The communication components
- Communication situations
- Communication realities

THE IMPORTANCE OF APPROPRIATE COMMUNICATION

Good communication skills offer individuals the opportunity to feel comfortable and confident in their ability to exchange their ideas in a timely, concise manner. It is also important to develop career speech that eliminates local dialects and grammar that occasionally prevent careers from maturing because an employee's language usage doesn't meet the demands of the employer's national/global, diverse clientele. Word selection when making a business presentation can tip the balance between a positive or negative reaction toward a presenter and the presentation itself. It is not enough to be educated and to know your academic area well; you must be able to present your thoughts professionally in spontaneous situations. Communication training assists career-seeking individuals with strategies to help them better present their ideas—and themselves. Business recruiters look for individuals with the communication skills to step into a position immediately as well as fit into the corporate environment with other employees.

On a personal level, we communicate in business to accomplish tasks, get things we want, negotiate a raise, conduct business conversations, meet people, function in teams, learn new concepts, and prove our value to an organization. A key strategy to being successful—and earning a satisfactory income—is to practice communication skills that assure others of your professionalism and your value to the company. The more effective you are in using language and professional behavior, the better the potential career outcome.

Business reports consistently list communication as one of the ten essential skills an employee should possess—typically one of the first three skills listed. The inclusion of communication skills is no accident when you consider the daily contact you have with colleagues: interpersonally, nonverbally, technically, socially, and in formal presentations. Professionalism involves improving your speaking style, behavior, written ability, and technical proficiency so business colleagues see you as someone who adds value to the company in addition to someone they want to retain during a corporate restructuring phase. Solid communication skills allow you to maneuver in the business world with self-confidence and a feeling of personal accomplishment.

COMMUNICATION COMPONENTS

Communication is an ongoing, cumulative process. For this reason, you need to polish every aspect of your communication prior to entering the business community. To be successful at communication, coworkers must effectively share meaning with one another. Sharing meaning involves one person comprehending the intended meaning of another person's language and nonverbal behavior. However, comprehension is challenging when you consider that another person's verbal style often evolves from their family background, education, culture, and ethnicity.

Nonverbal communication can be misinterpreted easily as well. Before you can fully understand communication complexities, you need to consider the elements that make up an ordinary interpersonal interaction. Every interaction consists of the following **communication components**: communicators, messages, a channel, circumstances, feedback, and, in some instances, noise. A good communicator analyzes each of these components prior to making the best possible language choices for each business interaction.

Communicators

Communicators are the people involved in a verbal/nonverbal/written exchange. Each individual simultaneously sends and receives messages. For example, a coworker who briefly stops by your office transmits both nonverbal (smiles, hand gestures, eye contact) and verbal messages (the task material he or she talks about). In addition, you send messages to your coworker by maintaining eye contact, writing notes, or even yawning during conversation. Everyone communicates something when they are in an environment with other people, whether or not they are aware of it. Effective communicators recognize that they intentionally and/or unintentionally send and receive messages; they constantly monitor and reflect on their verbal and nonverbal behavior as well as on the behavior of those around them while fine-tuning their skills. You can't control the communication style of another person, but you certainly can control and improve your own style to be perceived as a professional person.

For example, Laura notices that Rowan is distracted when she walks into the office. He is missing his usual quick smile and lively "good morning!" He is staring at the wall and belatedly utters a faint greeting after Laura reaches her desk. She perceives the difference in his usual nonverbal/verbal communication and proceeds based on that recognition. Laura sits at her desk and politely asks Rowan if something is wrong. His verbal and nonverbal responses to her question will dictate where their conversation goes next.

Messages

Messages can be either verbal or nonverbal. **Verbal messages** include all spoken language; **nonverbal messages** are actions or physical attributes without words. Nonverbal messages include our gestures, the way we use our voice (loud, soft, high or low pitch), the clothes we wear, the way we move, and the car we drive. When we enter an office, our clothes, gestures, haircut, personal possessions, or additional visual stimuli send nonverbal messages to colleagues. But remember, nonverbal messages have the potential to be decoded incorrectly by others. A handshake when meeting someone may be a polite gesture to you, but someone in a position of greater authority may see your action as inappropriate. Some individuals of higher status prefer to extend their hand first to initiate physical contact.

Verbal and nonverbal communication require the continuous encoding and decoding of messages. This process begins with a thought a person wishes to communicate. The person encodes the thought into words and/or physical actions. **Encoding** means a communicator reviews all of the available symbols (vocabulary) and/or actions that could best represent her thought and selects the most effective method of expression. Then, the person selects a channel to send those words or actions to other communicators. The other communicators receive the words or actions and decode the message prior to responding. **Decoding** means thinking about and reacting to received symbols or actions, applying meaning to them, and consolidating them into a usable thought for an appropriate response.

The more effective we are at encoding our thoughts, the more likely other communicators are able to decode the meaning of our messages properly. You will have a better chance for shared meaning and understanding in interpersonal and group situations when you employ good encoding and decoding skills. It is important for communicators to be aware that anyone can decode a meaning that wasn't intentional. For instance, someone might decode another's pause before speaking as, "the following statement is not true." However, communicators may pause simply because they are trying to find the best word choice to start the next phrase or sentence. We should constantly be aware that some of the meanings we decode could be inaccurate; thus we need to analyze messages thoroughly before responding.

In the business world, you may enhance language encoding by using professional jargon. **Jargon** is specialized language used to communicate within a specific field. For instance, in speech communication, we call overheads "visual aids" yet in the field of engineering, overheads have been called "view graphs." Camera operators call the horizontal movement of a camera lens a "pan," while to a performer a pan is a bad review and for a chef, something entirely different. Every profession uses its own jargon, and you must shift your use of jargon to accommodate understanding during professional communication. Using incorrect jargon signals a lack of experience working in a specific profession.

On the other hand, you must remember to eliminate technical jargon when you are talking to someone outside of your field of expertise. Your ability to flow in and out of jargon serves you well as long as you evaluate your intended audience. In other words, you can't use professional jargon when speaking to a community volunteer organization unrelated to your professional career. Language needs to target the background of an audience for them to clearly understand your message.

Delivery (how you say something) can enhance or hinder the effective decoding of a verbal message. The vocal characteristics we use in delivery include tone, pitch, rate, and variations in projection. All of these vocal characteristics color our words and phrases to emphasize or de-emphasize key thoughts in a presentation. If we don't deliver messages appropriately, our meaning may be distorted and decoded incorrectly by audience members.

Channels

Messages must travel through a specific medium to get from one communicator to another. We call these mediums channels. Each channel targets a different sensory receptor, so you must select the appropriate channel to accomplish your intended goal. The many **channels** include phones, handheld devices (iPhone, BlackBerry, pager, etc.), computers, websites, newspapers, radio, television, books, notes, blogs, Twitter, Facebook, sound systems, and face-to-face interaction.

When selecting a channel to deliver a message, remember that every communication situation necessitates an appropriate channel choice. For example, your department manager wants to fire your office mate, Anthony. She logs onto her computer and types, "The department is restructuring, and your position is terminated. Please clean out your desk by noon." She hits "send," then summons security to escort Anthony out of the building at noon. Is using e-mail an appropriate channel in this situation? What will Anthony think of her action? This may seem like an unlikely firing scenario; however, RadioShack fired 400 employees in 2006 by e-mail with a message that read, "The workforce reduction notification is currently in progress. Unfortunately, your position is one that has been eliminated" (Associated Press, 2006). Is e-mail ever a good choice for terminating employees? No matter how you view this choice, it is a reality in today's business environment.

Familiarity with navigating technical channels like websites, blogs, Twitter, Facebook, and texting prepare you for the contemporary workforce. Each technical channel uses specific jargon for communication. Companies use each of these channels to reach internal and external receivers. You need to move quickly from one channel to the next while maintaining the appropriate language required for each channel. Although the business world still uses traditional channels like letters and presentations, the increasing reliance on **technical convergence** (developing messages for multiple platforms) requires greater analysis and speed for targeting language to specific receivers.

When you choose a channel for various communication events, think about the purpose of the communication and the consequences of the message you send to make sure you have made the best decision. The appropriate channel can make a difference on how an audience receives a message. Some situations warrant direct involvement with the intended receiver of your message even though you may be more comfortable using a technical channel.

Many companies also monitor your public and social behavior as a reflection of their image in the community. In business, your communication can have positive or negative legal consequences, since you speak for the company as its employee. For example, if you are talking to a community group, they associate you with your employer. So make sure that when you are communicating via public channels, you always act in the best interest of the company. And keep any negative chatter about the company in a private channel.

Circumstances

Circumstances refer to the context of a communication situation and to the fundamental nature of the communicators, which includes a communicator's background, attitudes, beliefs, and values. All of these elements influence verbal and nonverbal message choices and reactions to messages when decoded. A heated discussion in a business meeting may be threatening to some colleagues and yet invigorating to others. The fundamental nature of each participant determines his or her personal reaction to a heated discussion.

The context of a circumstance also contributes to the meaning of a message. What you say in one situation may not be appropriate in a similar circumstance with different colleagues. Every circumstance and its participants are unique and call for targeted messages and responses. For example, you and your colleagues feel comfortable using jokes and calling each other names. In the context of your office environment, you are all satisfied with this banter. However, you may feel uncomfortable or be offended if someone from outside your group makes the same comments to you. Analyzing your circumstances, including your own fundamental nature and the context of a situation, allows you make appropriate choices before uttering a verbal response or reacting to a particular comment. Think carefully about whether previous communication choices apply to your current situation and respond accordingly.

Feedback

Feedback is the response one communicator gives to another. It can be verbal, nonverbal, or a combination of the two, but it is present in every interpersonal interaction. Feedback is essential during the communication process; it acknowledges the presence of the other person, lets the communicator know you received the message, and demonstrates that the communication is valued. For example, a simple gesture like leaving a colleague's favorite cup of coffee on his or her desk as you return from a personal break signals that you appreciate sharing the workload. Your colleague may never return the favor, but you have communicated a team-oriented approach.

You can improve your feedback by remembering to be timely. Responding to someone as soon as possible regarding a message so that they don't have to track you down helps to improve your business credibility. There are times when the sender can perceive any delay by the receiver as an inability to answer a question or as an avoidance tactic.

Immediacy behaviors are another key component to being perceived as a friendly employee. People who smile and look attentive, have positive body posture, and lean toward the other person when someone is talking are perceived to be giving positive feedback that keeps the conversation going. Obviously, sometimes you don't want to give that impression, but being open and friendly in your nonverbal feedback in general will help you to appear engaged and as if you are listening and interested.

Noise/Distractions

Noise consists of any distractions that interrupt communicators from encoding, sending, receiving, and/or decoding a message properly. There are three types of noise you need to consider as you communicate: physical, personal, and semantic.

Physical noise.   Any external, distracting sound present during communication, from a humming light fixture to a bug flying around your desk while you are editing a document, constitutes physical noise. Physical noise distracts us and competes with our thought processes. As a communicator, you must concentrate harder on your remarks to avoid the external distraction whether you are speaking or writing. This is one reason why we turn down the car radio while trying to locate a client's office for the first time. It's easier to concentrate on your driving and spot a location when physical noise is minimized.

Personal noise.   Personal noise refers to ongoing thoughts or concerns in our minds. There are three types of personal noise that can distract our attention while focusing on a task:

- Prejudice
- Closed-mindedness
- Self-centeredness

Prejudice.   Prejudice occurs when we "pre-judge" or have a preconceived, often negative, view of someone or something. If, for example, you have biases against public school education, you may have a negative impression regarding the intellectual ability of anyone trained in a public environment. If you learn a colleague is from a public university, you may underestimate his or her ability. Conversely, if you are prejudiced toward private education, you could overestimate the ability of a colleague trained in a private environment. You should always be aware of personal prejudices and choose to eliminate them as you evaluate messages, people, and situations. Failure to do so could result in costly mistakes for your career.

Closed-mindedness.   Closed-mindedness occurs when we refuse to listen to another person's point of view. Think about your position on a topic like the virtual office: employees working from their home. Chances are you feel very strongly about the topic. Could you learn something by hearing information from the opposing side? Of course you can. However, many people who believe they are right or know the truth refuse to listen to any information that conflicts with their own beliefs. This rigidity harms the communication process. In business, you could easily get into a heated discussion about such a topic. If you are arguing closed-mindedly, you could destroy another person's confidence in your ability to be reasonable and fair.

Self-centeredness.   Self-centered noise occurs when we focus more on ourselves than on the other person during communication. How often do you zone out in meetings thinking about your own schedule, a meeting you have in two hours, your weekend activities, the party you attended the night before, or even what you will have for dinner? You may have learned the art of smiling, nodding and/or looking attentive during a presentation even though you are not paying the least bit of attention to the message. This personal distraction can easily lead to making a serious mistake at work (for example, failing to use a new technical protocol discussed at the department meeting). This attention failure can cost you your position. While you may have been able to zone out in college lectures and get by, you'll need to change this behavior to succeed in business.

Semantic noise.   The third type of noise is semantic noise. Semantic noise occurs when the person you are communicating with speaks a different language, uses technical jargon, and/or resorts to emotionally charged words. As the corporate sector expands globally, the potential for problems caused by different languages increases. Some of your colleagues may not use English as effectively as you do, just as you may not use their language as effectively as they do. Now, add technical jargon to your communication, which is also confusing. If one communicator knows the terminology and the other does not, sharing meaning is difficult if not impossible.

Emotionally charged words also block the communication process. The listener may fixate on a word rather than paying attention to the complete message. For example, in some regions of the United States, the terms "Ma'am" and "Sir" refer to people who are in positions of authority, even if they are only 30 years old. However, in other areas of the United States, those terms conjure up images of senior citizens. The term "Ma'am" might offend a 30-year-old woman in northern California—just as a 30-year-old woman in Arkansas could be offended if a younger person didn't use "Ma'am" while addressing her. Business language should always be respectful; effective business language involves knowing the customs of a particular locale and adapting to its style.

Every step of the communication process is important in establishing your credibility with others. Select your message and channel carefully. As a communicator, you must be aware of the entire chain of events your words or actions initiate and accept responsibility for the choices you make throughout a conversation. Always consider the circumstances of the people around you as you evaluate a message and select the appropriate channel for its delivery. You should be aware of noise in every interaction and work to eliminate it whenever possible. And you should do your best to provide proper feedback to the requests of colleagues. These personal communication choices make professional interactions as smooth and effective as possible. To be an effective communicator, you should strive to make wiser verbal and nonverbal choices as you become more aware of how interactive the process truly is.

Post-analysis of every interaction can help you evaluate a poor communication experience: "Was it me?" "Was it the other person?" "Was it the channel?" "Was my message worded incorrectly?" "Was there noise?" The answers to all of these questions will help you pinpoint problem areas and allow you to make appropriate corrections in future communication. Examining personal word/behavioral choices that work or don't work allow you to improve future interactions.

COMMUNICATION SITUATIONS

There are four basic communication situations.

- Intrapersonal communication: communicating within yourself

- Interpersonal communication: communicating with another person

- Small group communication: communicating with 3–20 people (with 5–8 as the ideal size) who have a common goal

- Public communication: communicating with a large audience

When we mentally review, rehearse, or analyze conversations or experiences internally, we are engaging in **intrapersonal communication**. Think how often you do a mental review of content or organizational structure prior to an important meeting or presentation. Before you meet with a manager, do you think about what you are going to say in the time given to you? When your alarm goes off in the morning, do you think, "If I hit the snooze button, I can give up the shower, sleep for another 18 minutes, and wear a hat"? We use intrapersonal communication constantly as we meditate, reflect, and strategize. Intrapersonal communication helps us to know ourselves, to practice important communication scenarios, to analyze everything around us (including our own actions), and to think critically of past and future events.

In contrast to the internal dialogue of intrapersonal communication, **interpersonal communication** takes place whenever two people speak or see one another in addition to a written exchange of ideas, no matter how brief the exchange.

Recall the discussion you had with a coworker about office expenses; the complaints you shared with someone about an office colleague; the person you acknowledged in the cafeteria; a boss you spoke to regarding a raise. You should be able to list at least 50 exchanges you had with others in the last 24 hours. We use interpersonal communication constantly to help create and maintain our relationships: personal and public. These relationships reflect our professional image.

Interpersonal communication becomes **small group communication** when the number of people expands slightly; groups typically have 3–20 members. Group members share a general sense of belonging and usually share common beliefs, goals, or reasons for getting together. Group members work together to accomplish task, organizational, and/or relationship goals.

Groups with task goals meet to solve a problem or complete an assignment. You can find this type of group in the workplace or in volunteer organizations. Task groups normally consist of five to eight people. When your company asks five of you to develop a marketing plan for the distribution a new product, you are a part of a task group. Another function of groups is the relationship goal, which fulfills the personal needs of conversation and belonging. These groups may consist of close friends who eat dinner together occasionally or colleagues who go to a movie at the end of the week simply to unwind. Sometimes groups have both task and relationship goals. These blended groups could include a social group, book club, and/or a religious gathering. In addition to relationship functions, these groups also perform tasks such as fundraisers, social service projects, reading assignments, and so forth.

Teams are a specific type of small group. Teams work on tasks designed to accomplish a specific goal. Members of teams employ a standard procedure to accomplish their goal. Teams are prevalent in numerous workplace environments. In this text, we focus exclusively on communication within teams rather than on the broader concept of small group communication because solid teamwork results in job satisfaction, overall productivity, and personal fulfillment and responsibility.

Public communication occurs when a communicator informs, persuades, and/or entertains a large group of people. Speakers have an organized message to deliver, an official audience, and they prepare for an event. Typically, public communication comes in the form of training seminars, oral presentations, a keynote address at a conference, and corporate announcements via in-house media, as well as messages delivered through digital media. You may think you will never have to give a speech after graduating from college; however, public communication is definitely in your future. You should learn the skills for effective public speaking so that you are better prepared when opportunities arise in both your professional and personal life. Once you have employment, your public performance reflects on your employer. You should always deliver the presentations you make with superior performance standards. Professional success is more probable when you function at your best consistently.

COMMUNICATION REALITIES

Improving your communication skills takes time, practice, and dedication. It involves thinking before acting, research, making the best verbal and nonverbal choices for public behavior, and dealing responsibly with the consequences of those choices. Below are four principles to keep in mind when thinking about communication.

- We cannot not communicate
- Communication is irreversible
- Communication is an ongoing, cumulative process
- Communication involves ethical considerations

We cannot not communicate.   Someone, somewhere, receives and interprets everything we do. Even if we isolate ourselves, thinking we won't have to communicate, the very act of not interacting with people you've known for a long time communicates a specific message to them. We communicate with family members, friends, coworkers, peers, professors, salespersons, significant others, and many more. We constantly put our communication skills to the test every minute of every day.

Communication is irreversible—whether it is intentional or unintentional.   If you say something or do something that upsets another person, you can't change it. Once the words are out of your mouth or you complete an inappropriate action, the damage is done. You can apologize and hope to lessen the impact of your words or behaviors, but you can't change the initial impression you made. When you choose certain words or act a certain way, there are consequences: some positive and some negative. Effective communicators understand this principle and, therefore, think carefully before they speak or act. They monitor and reflect on all of their communication.

Communication is an ongoing, cumulative process.   The bits of information we collect internally become part of our fundamental nature and affect our future communication. By being more aware of why we say the things we do, we can improve our professional speech style and learn numerous new diverse perspectives. We each experience the world a little differently, so in addition to understanding and improving our own style, we need to remember that other people have their own unique style as well. No one is a perfect communicator; instead, we have varying degrees of success in different situations. Effective communicators are flexible because they adapt their messages to the circumstances they encounter. Improving your communication skills is a life-long commitment to building an excellent professional image. You already possess basic communication skills; by increasing your performance repertoire (verbal, nonverbal, written, and use of technical channels), you will be able to handle the numerous diverse situations you encounter daily. You don't need to imitate others or to compromise your values and ethical standards to be successful. However, polishing language skills allows you to communicate effectively and to adjust to unexpected circumstances.

Communication involves ethical considerations as well.   As you think about the fact that communication is an ongoing process and that it is irreversible, you want to think about its ethical considerations.

"Ethical issues may arise in human behavior whenever that behavior could have significant impact on other persons, when the behavior involves conscious choice of means and ends, and when the behavior can be judged by standards of right and wrong" (Johannesen, Valde, and Whedbee, 2008, p. 1). You will find ethical questions to consider/analyze beginning in chapter 2. These ethical issues provide opportunities for reflection and for discussion with your classmates.

Many communication situations we face on a daily basis in business include ethical choices. For example, do we pass along a piece of gossip we hear about a peer? Or do we take the time to investigate the comment prior to making a decision regarding its truthfulness and passing it along? Or do we refrain from sharing the information altogether? On another day, do we refrain from communicating that we disagree with a policy decision? Or do we hide our feelings by remaining silent? Each of these choices has considerable ethical consequences related to your credibility and professional judgment.

We can also use communication to uphold personal ethics and moral standards in everyday life. We do so, for instance, in a grocery store when we inform the clerk that the register undercharged us, or when we tell a server that the dessert we ordered is missing from the bill. Our conduct projects our personal ethical standards to those around us in these daily situations.

The better you know yourself through intrapersonal examination, and the more you practice communicating interpersonally, the better equipped you will be to handle challenging business situations.

FINAL THOUGHTS

Someone is always observing your behavior, listening to your communication style, and analyzing your abilities. Their judgments are cumulative and, in numerous professional situations, never revealed to you. Professional advancement is rooted in judgments that others make about you and your abilities on a daily basis. Therefore, you should do your best to be consistent with your language and behavior at all times. The knowledge you gain from this book will help you to review and to improve your current skills so that you become a more successful communicator in a variety of situations. Every new situation is as simple and as complicated as walking into your office space on the first day of a new job while being evaluated by colleagues. Chapter 2 will help you analyze your communication and behavior so that you will be more aware of your fundamental nature as you continue your journey toward becoming a business professional.

KEY TERMS

Channel	Messages (verbal/nonverbal)
Circumstances	Noise
Close-mindedness	Personal noise
Communication components	Physical noise
Communicators	Prejudice
Decoding	Public communication
Encoding	Self-centeredness
Feedback	Semantic noise
Interpersonal communication	Small group communication
Intrapersonal communication	Teams
Jargon	Technical convergence

EXERCISES

1. Divide the class into small groups. Each group will build and maintain a weekly blog discussing and updating the material in the book as it's covered.

2. Research a current business publication online to find a Top 10 list of the skills professionals feel are necessary to obtain a job. How many of the skills listed are communication skills? Why are these skills important to a corporation?

3. What are your strongest and weakest communication skills? How can you improve your weakest skill?

4. What channel do you prefer for most communication? Why? What channel do you like least? Why?

5. What communication challenges are present when addressing someone twenty or more years older? Discuss the differences in addressing a parent versus an employer the same age as the parent.

6. Wear professional attire to each class for a week. Does you attire change the way you feel?

2

Intrapersonal Examination

GOALS

After reading this chapter you should be able to:

✓ Describe the three steps of the perceptual process

✓ Analyze the differences in people's varying perceptions

✓ Practice the perception checking skill

✓ Explain how perception relates to self-concept and self-esteem

✓ Choose and rank values that are important to you

✓ Assess your strengths and weaknesses

✓ Assess your intrapersonal qualities

✓ Appraise your communication skills, predict your success, and plan for improvements

As you begin to think about a career, it is important to have a thorough understanding of yourself. You need to be able to assess your job skills, communication skills, personal values, qualities, and goals. What kind of person are you? Does your perception of who you are match the perception strangers have of you? What career do you want to pursue? Do your answers to these basic questions about yourself match the qualifications for the career you've selected?

The world of technology has everyone talking, befriending total strangers, tweeting and blogging, but few individuals are really looking at or analyzing the motivation behind message exchanges. Effective communicators allow verbal and nonverbal messages to be a true reflection of who they are and what they think; it is extremely important to know who you really are. On a personal level, are you energetic, lazy, enthusiastic, boring, innovative, or dull? Are you a needy person or extremely independent? Do you take charge of a situation or drag your feet in making decisions? The answers to all of these questions are extremely important to consider as you prepare for your working career. Professional people should project a credible image by consistently matching verbal and nonverbal messages with what they know to be true about themselves.

Imagine attending a department meeting in which you and your colleagues are locked in a heated, hour-long discussion with your boss. The discussion is extremely direct. As you return to your desk after the meeting, a colleague remarks about what an invigorating discussion it was while another colleague is visibly shaken, feeling he was the target of yelling. How can two colleagues react so differently to the same meeting? Although both participated actively in the discussion, they did not perceive the session's significance in the same way. It is useful to remember that personal **perception** is more than its dictionary definition: the influence of visual stimuli. Chapter 1 discussed the term "fundamental nature." It is an important term to keep in the back of your mind during all of your communication with others. Because people have different experiences as well as expectations, they perceive events and personal behaviors differently. Competent communicators understand that perception affects how individuals encode and decode messages and are savvy enough to assess potential communication difficulty due to perceptual differences in every public exchange.

THE PERCEPTUAL PROCESS

You are asked to attend a meeting to discuss financial restraint. You need to keep departmental expenses at a minimal level for the next two fiscal quarters. Employees must find a way to slash the current operating budget by 20% or management will have to lay off someone. Everyone attending the meeting is apprehensive about how to manage current departmental responsibilities and duties with such a significant financial decrease while trying to save everyone's position. Tom suggests that the department limit photocopying; Shareese immediately raises her voice to oppose the idea. She is uneasy with his suggestion because photocopying is an extremely important part of her business routine. If she can't have unlimited photocopying, she will not be able to meet her clients' needs. Shareese is quite assertive and not afraid to voice her opinion. Kay, a quiet young woman, perceives her boisterous communication style as "attitude" and feels that Shareese is yelling at group members even though Shareese feels she is simply defending her position. The varying reactions of individual employees reveal the perceptual differences in collegial fundamental nature. Everyone's differing perception of how a verbal discussion should be conducted makes professional communication challenging.

Another colleague, Rick, considers what he could do without but doesn't share his ideas. He isn't really paying attention to the comments of Tom, Shareese, or Kay. A little later however, Shareese makes a snide remark to Tom regarding Rick's unwillingness to enter the discussion seriously. Her zinger is somewhat funny but also hurtful. Na'eem overhears the remark and smiles; Kay is totally unaware of the exchange. Rick has a negative personal reaction to Shareese's remark because it reminds him of how his wife snipes at him at home. The tone of the discussion begins to shift as Rick allows his negative reaction to her remark to color his professional judgment and subsequent communication.

The personal perceptions of each individual in the scenario above influence and affect the behavior of each, making it difficult to remain focused on the topic itself. The **perceptual process** occurs in three stages: (1) selection; (2) organization; and (3) interpretation (McGaan, 2003). In the first step of the perceptual process—**selection**—your mind decides which of the numerous distractions during communication to recognize.

Rick hears Shareese's snide remark, while Kay does not. Kay notices Shareese's tone of voice, which Tom doesn't consider threatening in any way. Tom notices that Kay is withdrawing nonverbally, shrinking physically by slouching in the chair and crossing her arms, but no one else pays attention to her nonverbal behavioral shift.

Meanwhile, there are other distractions (physical noise) in the room that no one notices: the coffee maker is dripping, the fluorescent light is humming, and street noise is swirling in through an open window. If we acknowledged all of the sensory stimuli around us, we'd be overwhelmed and have trouble concentrating on the tasks in front of us.

Perception helps us sort through external stimuli for relevance as we focus on the task(s) in front of us. The process of focusing on specific stimuli (language, behavior, sound, color, temperature, etc.) and ignoring everything else is called **selective attention**. While numerous other stimuli are present in every environment, we normally focus on the primary tasks before us (although personal reactions may color our perceptions) while eliminating secondary distractions.

In the second step of the perceptual process—**organization**—your brain takes the stimuli you receive and organizes them by mentally grouping them together in meaningful, organized ways. Recently we received the following anonymous e-mail:

> aoccdrnig to a rscheeahcr at an Elingsh uinervtisy, it deosn't mttaer in waht oredr the ltteers in a wrod are, the olny iprmoetnt tihng is that frist and lsat ltteer is at the rghit pclae. The rset can be a toatl mses and you can sitll raed it wouthit porbelm. Tihs is bcuseae we do not raed ervey lteter by itslef but the wrod as a wlohe.

This e-mail example demonstrates how quickly our minds analyze and reorganize information. Almost everyone can read the paragraph above with little or no trouble at all. Our minds also fill in blanks/errors as we read and listen. If you receive a partial message, you fill in the holes in written language automatically. Although this is an amazing ability of the brain, you should be very careful in professional communication to make sure your written material is accurate. Even though someone may not notice a mistake because they "fill in" your error perceptually, you can't count on that. In addition, it is doubly hard to proofread material because your mind corrects the errors. Proofreading everything you write for accurate spelling and grammar sends a clear signal to others of your competence and credibility in communication.

We organize the relevance of messages by comparing them to information we retain from previous experiences. Thinking about similar situations, incidences, or behaviors allows us to use them to categorize new information prior to assigning meaning. It's frequently assumed that future events in our lives possess similarities to previous experiences. This assumption helps us select and organize stimuli for a response, but it can also limit our ability to perceive new information properly. When we fail to view new perceptual input with an open mind, it is difficult to be an effective communicator. We may recognize only similarities rather than noticing subtle nuances of difference in the new input. Previous judgments can be a guide to selecting good language/behavior responses, but they can also easily cloud our willingness to remain open to analyzing new information properly when we feel rushed to make a decision.

Once you organize stimuli by grouping it into categories and comparing it to your previous experiences, you move into the third step of the perceptual process—**interpretation and response**. You interpret all stimuli you receive and assign meaning to it. This third step is where you reflect your fundamental nature. Every influence from your home, family, community, religious establishment, your learning experiences, relationships, and so on play a role in how you interpret a specific perceptual event and respond to it verbally and nonverbally.

Let's return to the business meeting in which you are participating: Rick's cell phone rings, and he decides to answer it. You pay attention to the call for a moment and then become annoyed because you perceive that Rick thinks the business meeting is less important than his incoming call. That is the meaning you assign to Rick's nonverbal communication. Your attention shifts away from him once again after a brief period and returns to the financial conversation, but you remain very annoyed with Rick based on your perceptual interpretation of his lack of cell phone etiquette. However, others don't interpret Rick's act in the same way.

VARYING PERCEPTIONS

People's perceptions of the same sensory input are not identical for a variety of reasons. For example, let's revisit the cell phone incident at the business meeting. You perceive Rick's actions as offensive, while Tom is busy eavesdropping. He perceives the call as a welcome distraction from the heated, cost-cutting discussion. Kay is glad to have something else to focus on other than Shareese's shrill comments. Na'eem is the youngest colleague in the room, and he grew up using a cell phone and new media. He perceives the phone interruption as necessary. He is comfortable answering a cell phone no matter when it rings because he can handle multiple conversations and respond appropriately.

So why do perceptions vary? How can two individuals assign meaning differently when they experience the same stimuli? Think back to the communication process and our discussion of circumstances. We talked about the fact that all the participants in the communication possess different backgrounds and experiences. As you add that personal component to the perceptual process, you can begin to appreciate the complexities of communication. In the organizing step, we are comparing sensory stimuli to our past experiences. When people have different experiences, it is reasonable to deduce that they can have different interpretations for stimuli while engaged in interpersonal communication. Therefore, it is important to make sure that others clearly understand your communication style.

The concept of perception applies not only to individuals but also to departments within companies as well as businesses. Professionals can brand a specific department in their own organization as ineffective: troublesome personalities, don't meet deadlines, don't keep promises, do shoddy work, etc. If you wind up working in such a department, your corporate colleagues may automatically consider you to have poor skills because you are part of the "bad" department. Changing the perception of an entire department within a company is a daunting task and may never occur. Even in business, perception can override reality.

PERCEPTION CHECKING

Because the interpretation phase of communication leaves us vulnerable to misunderstanding, perception checking is a skill you can use to double-check your comprehension of what is going on with another person. **Perception checking** consists of three parts:

- First, you give an objective description of what you sensed

- Second, you give an interpretation of what the situation meant to you

- Finally, you ask a question to clarify for accurate meaning

In the previous example, you could say to Rick, "I noticed you answered your cell phone during the meeting. I feel that is disruptive and shows that you are not interested in the department's future. Is this the case?" This is truly a textbook example of perception checking. No one really speaks this way, however. So how could you rephrase those thoughts in a way that still follows the three steps, but sounds more natural? The goal of perception checking is clarity. You could try, "Hey Rick, I see you kept getting calls during the meeting. Do you have an important deal that you need to finalize?"

It is useful to remember that you should only use perception checking if there is a chance your attribution of meaning is incorrect. For example, it would be inappropriate to use perception checking in the following example:

Kay: Na'eem, would you please close the door so we can avoid distractions?

Na'eem: I'm getting the sense you would like to have the door closed. Would you?

It is also inappropriate to overuse perception checking. Think of how annoying it would be to have someone constantly checking to see if you are mad at them. Sometimes people use perception checking inappropriately as a communication tool for conversational clarity when they really need to simply stop and think for a minute about the communication. In our initial example of the communication differences between Shareese and Kay, if Shareese is speaking in an excited or intense voice, why is Kay's first perception that Shareese is yelling (angry)? Why wouldn't Kay assume Shareese feels strongly about the topic? Some people tend to think that everything is their fault when in reality they need to think of other possible reasons that might trigger another person's behavior.

You should use perception checking when you truly want to understand what is going on with another person. If a colleague is in a bad mood and you work closely with her, you can choose to ignore her language or behavior and stay out of her way until her mood improves. But if a situation continues to bother you, and you need to clarify whether you are the cause of her foul mood before simply assuming you are, then use perception checking as a tool of resolution. Something else could be on the other person's mind.

In the business world, however, you can't always figure out the dynamics of every interaction. Sometimes people say hurtful things, and you simply need to move on. What if you perception check with someone, and he says that he had no hurtful intentions. He was resolving another situation in his mind, and didn't think before saying something to you. However, you still feel hurt. There is no easy way to resolve this. Some people want everyone to know when they are hurt or offended by words or actions. This response is not perception checking, because it does not ask for communication clarity. The response is an emotional reaction asking for an apology, not clarity. The fact is, some business people care if they've hurt your feelings, and others simply don't care at all. You need to know your emotional self well before you ask for clarity from others. You may be perceived as emotionally weak if you are constantly offended by colleagues. This perception could prevent promotion within an organization as well as lead to your removal. As part of an intrapersonal assessment, you need to ask yourself how often you feel hurt by another person's remarks or actions. Can you take constructive criticism and fix the problem, or do you perceive any criticism to be malicious or hurtful (they don't like me)? Why?

ETHICAL ENCOUNTERS

There are moments in a professional career when you can use perception checking to reveal personal beliefs and/or principles. You must determine within yourself if a personal principle is worth revealing as you ask someone for clarity. In other words, what are the consequences for your future? For example, it is definitely worth asking, "I'm not sure what you mean by that?" if someone makes a racist, sexist, or homophobic remark. If they respond with an "Awww come on, I was just joking around!" you may need to reply with a request, "Ok, please don't talk that way around me." This response clearly lets the other person know how you wish to be treated. But if the remark is a small, inconsequential one about a situation at work or the disorder on your desk, it may be best to ignore the remark and move on. If you call attention to the remark, you will enhance its significance for yourself and the other person will remember you for speaking up. Each of you alters your perception of the other based on the remark, and an off-hand interaction will influence all future communication with each other. What principles do you hold that are worth perception checking?

Finally, there are many people who feel awkward using the perception-checking skill. It does take some practice if you haven't used it a great deal. Some people are reluctant to use perception checking because it is easier to assume what another person means than to ask for clarity. You may think you will appear to be weak if you ask for clarity. Although asking someone to explain his or her behavior may be initially awkward, the value of accuracy in communication—personal and professional—is immeasurable.

PERCEPTION RELATED TO SELF-CONCEPT

Another way perception relates to each of us is through its connection to self-concept. **Self-concept** refers to what we think about ourselves (positive and negative), including our physical attributes (short or tall, big or small), our aptitudes (good managerial skills, getting along with others), our physical coordination (good athlete, proficient at yoga), our skills (creativity, analytical reasoning), and our knowledge of a specialty area (computer programming, graphic design). Most of these attributes are factual personal assessments. We recognize whether we are tall or short, good at interpersonal relationships, type 100 wpm, speak well, write well, and so forth. These conclusions are the result of intrapersonal assessment and evaluation.

Some people, however, cannot accurately assess themselves. They think they are talented at things when they are actually deficient, or they are hypercritical of themselves even when they are good at what they do. While being confident and/or humble are both terrific qualities, accurate **self-assessment** allows you to interact with others without being annoying. No one wants to listen to a braggart or a whiner.

We also assess ourselves through comments others make about us, or our perceptions of their nonverbal reaction to us. Personal evaluations made by teachers, family members, significant others, friends, siblings, other relatives, coaches, and religious leaders impact our sense of self, and they need to be analyzed for accuracy in order to improve on weaknesses we perceive as valid. If, as a child, you hear someone say that you are "pretty" or "smart" or "stupid" or "lazy," these verbal labels shape your perception of yourself. Nicknames such as "chubby," "slim," "bubba," or "princess" also affect self-concept. If we see ourselves through the labels given to us by others, we may develop a self-concept based on illusion rather than reality. These labels can influence the way you present yourself to business colleagues as an adult. Do you see yourself as a "Bubba" on the way to a job interview? Do you see yourself as a "princess?" If so, how will the human resources director evaluate these perceptions? It is better to see yourself as professionally qualified rather than as a Bubba or princess to market yourself appropriately.

Placing too much value on labels from others can be problematic. If you were unlucky enough to have verbally abusive parents who constantly told you that you were incapable of doing anything right, you need to make sure that you don't live up to the negative label they placed on you. People, even parents, can be mean and wrong. Someone else's opinion is simply that . . . an opinion—it is not a fact.

Naturally, self-concept influences your communication skills with the external world. Our presentational style, use of nonverbal communication, ability to interact on an interpersonal level, or our ability to function in a team environment evolves from our self-concept. If our self-concept is one of shyness, we are likely to have non-animated non-verbals, a quiet disposition and subdued presentational style, and we may be reluctant to participate in teams. On the other hand, if our self-concept is one of confidence, we stand tall, speak effectively (grammar and tone), and willingly participate in teams.

Before you venture into the business world, it is important to have a realistic grasp of your self-concept to avoid placing yourself in professional situations you are not prepared to handle. During the intrapersonal evaluation process, write a description of yourself centering on the various aspects of self-concept. What are your strengths and weaknesses? Once you examine your self-concept truthfully, you can begin to strengthen each skill you possess and to correct your perceived weaknesses.

PERCEPTION RELATED TO SELF-ESTEEM

Self-esteem refers to the value we place on our self-concept while observing and interacting with the environment around us. For example, part of Rachel's self-concept is that she's fairly short because she is only 5′1″ tall. Her self-esteem related to this concept depends on the value she places on height. In U.S. culture, research shows that tall people have an advantage over competitors in interviews, presidential elections, and promotions (Andersen, 2008, pp. 320–321). If Rachel thinks only tall people are attractive and competent, her self-esteem will probably be low because there is nothing she can do to change her height. However, if she believes competency does not depend on height, then being 5′1″ tall will not affect her self-esteem as she interacts with other people.

Sometimes, it is easy to be your own worst enemy. However, you can choose to be either extremely critical or extremely supportive of yourself. How you communicate intrapersonally affects your self-esteem. What do you say to yourself when you miss a project deadline? Do you say, "I can't believe how stupid I am! I can never do anything right." This negative internal communication can damage your self-esteem and affect future behavior. Or, do you say something positive to yourself, "Wow. I can't believe I didn't make that deadline. I need to figure out what to do differently so I can improve my performance and keep this job." The differences in these two approaches to intrapersonal communication can harm or improve self-esteem. It is important to remain positive in self-criticism, so you can solve your problem(s) and improve performance.

Self-esteem and self-concept influence our willingness and ability to communicate effectively. If you feel good about yourself, you are more likely to meet new people, to assert your ideas in a team situation, to stand confidently before an audience as you speak, and to experiment with new communication strategies. If you don't trust yourself to discover new inner abilities and instead rely only on past skills that make you feel comfortable, you constrict personal growth and hinder potential marketability. If you feel you need to strengthen your self-concept or self-esteem, there are numerous books and articles outlining steps to practice. You may also want to seek professional assistance if necessary. Thorough awareness of both concepts (self-concept and self-esteem) is extremely useful before venturing into the workplace.

VALUES, PERSONAL QUALITIES (SKILLS), AND COMMUNICATION ASSESSMENTS

In addition to understanding the concept of perception and how it relates to your self-concept and self-esteem, you should also do some work assessing your values, personal qualities and skills, and communication skills.

Values

The first thing to do in your assessment of self is to take a serious look at the things you value. Matching your **values** to a potential job will help you make better employment decisions. A career is challenging enough; working in an environment that doesn't match your personal values will increase the difficulty. There are a number of different values and numerous lists to research for assistance. The one that follows offers a good start in assessing your personal values (Roberts, n.d.). Underline the words that are important to you; review the values you underlined and circle the five that are the most important to you. Discuss your choices with classmates and look for similarities and differences.

Achievement	Financial gain	Physical challenge
Advancement and promotion	Freedom	Pleasure
Adventure	Friendships	Power and authority
Affection (love and caring)	Growth	Privacy
Arts	Having a family	Public service
Being around people who are open and honest	Helping other people	Purity
Challenging problems	Helping society	Quality of what I take part in
Change and variety	Honesty	Quality relationships
Close relationships	Independence	Recognition (respect from others, status)
Community	Influencing others	Religion
Competence	Inner harmony	Reputation
Competition	Integrity	Responsibility and accountability
Cooperation	Intellectual status	Security
Country	Involvement	Self-respect
Creativity	Job tranquility	Serenity
Decisiveness	Knowledge	Sophistication
Democracy	Leadership	Stability
Ecological awareness	Location	Status
Economic security	Loyalty	Supervising others
Effectiveness	Market position	Time freedom
Efficiency	Meaningful work	Truth
Ethical practice	Merit	Wealth
Excellence	Money	Wisdom
Excitement	Nature	Work under pressure
Fame	Order (tranquility, stability, conformity)	Work with others
Fast living	Personal development	Working alone

What is the most important value you possess according to the list you just created? Does the business you are interested in match your personal values? For instance, if money is your number one value, then you may be willing to work under pressure, supervise others, and place your family second to the job. On the other hand, if family is the most important thing to you, you may need to realize that you can't have a fast-paced, travel-filled, high-pressure job that keeps you at the office at all hours or on-call.

If you accept a job at a company with values significantly different from your own, you may regret the decision eventually. For example, we knew someone who went to work at a huge corporation. It seemed like a dream job with a clothing allowance, a high salary, and lots of prestige. However, our friend soon realized that the company expected him to be available for any and all events. There were mandatory happy hours, mandatory golf weekends, etc. He soon found that his time was not his own, not to mention he hated golf. The company paid time-and-a-half for these events, but soon even the money wasn't that valuable anymore. Our friend valued his independence and alone time. He discovered he had to leave the company after only 9 months; more importantly, he discovered that his initial assessment of money as his most important value was inaccurate. He found that he valued himself more than the money he was making. Thus, he approached his next employment possibility with a much more realistic evaluation of himself.

Personal values can shift with time and experience. This is not a frustrating concept or an example of personal failure. It simply indicates personal and professional adjustment as you gain experience and more self-awareness. Periodic self-examination highlights possible changes and corresponding shifts in emphasis.

ETHICAL ENCOUNTERS

What happens when you encounter others in the workplace whose values differ from your own? How will you handle that situation?

Personal Qualities (Skills)

Before you go looking for a new job, it is important to figure out how good you are at what you want to do. If you've been actively preparing for your career, you've done an internship in your area of interest as a student, part-time work that supports your career choice, or volunteer work to beef up your résumé and to gain experience working with others. For example, are you knowledgeable about the software listed in the job ad? Are you comfortable in diverse situations? Can you plan large social events? Do you consistently send thank you notes to people who make a difference in your daily routine? In other words, how complete are your **personal qualities/skills**?

Julie Jansen (2010), a career coach and counselor, identifies 11 keys to success that any individual can develop. These are all qualities that help us to be successful people.

1. **Confidence:** belief in oneself based on a realistic understanding of one's capabilities and circumstances

2. **Curiosity:** an eagerness to know and learn; exhibiting constant interest; paying special attention to the less obvious

3. **Decisiveness:** making a choice and taking action

4. **Empathy:** seeking to understand someone else's feelings and situation; demonstrating caring

5. **Flexibility:** responding positively to change; being adaptable and able to deal with ambiguity

6. **Humor:** not taking yourself too seriously; being amusing and amused; viewing the world with enjoyment

7. **Intelligence:** thinking and planning before acting; working efficiently (Jansen stresses that this skill differs from one's IQ)

8. **Optimism:** focusing on the positive aspects of a situation; expecting good outcomes

9. **Perseverance:** persistence and hard work with passion, energy, and focus to achieve results

10. **Respect:** treating others considerately and courteously; protecting the self-esteem of others

11. **Self-awareness:** monitoring and observing yourself; consciously changing your thought processes and behaviors

How many of the 11 qualities do you possess? What steps could you take to improve some of the qualities you consider weak? Awareness of each quality can assist you in strengthening your ability to project these skills to others, but remember that you want people to perceive the attributes as genuine. Coaches/mentors can help individuals develop the desirable qualities, which is why people often use the terms "qualities" and "skills" interchangeably.

Communication Skills

The final assessment you should do concerns your verbal and nonverbal **communication skills**. Communication skills are often hard to assess yourself, so be sure to ask others around you about specific concerns. There are many self-assessment instruments on the Internet that you can use as a checklist. We have included a brief assessment instrument below that should get you started thinking about the communication skills you may have.

ETHICAL ENCOUNTERS

How ethical is it to say that you have good communication skills when in fact, you do not?

Communication Skills Self-Assessment Exercise

Answering questions about your own communication skills is somewhat difficult since personal perception can be different from reality. To best analyze yourself, answer the questions and then ask a trusted friend and/or colleague if they think that your answers are accurate. Remember that you can work to change any area of communication weakness if you choose to do so.

1. Is your nonverbal communication appropriate for business and appealing to others? Think specifically about your handshake, eye contact, and your facial expression.

   My nonverbal communication is:

| Excellent | Sufficient | ✕ Needs Work | Embarrassing |

[When someone meets you, they will immediately notice a firm and confident handshake, direct and appropriate (not creepy) eye contact, and a pleasant and approachable facial expression. If you do these things well, you increase your chances of a good first impression.]

---

2. Do you have the confidence and initiative to introduce yourself to people in the office if your boss does not do so?

    My communication initiative to make a solid first impression is:

Excellent   ✳ **Sufficient**   **Needs work**   **Embarrassing**

[In many companies, someone will take you around and introduce you to colleagues, but in other companies you are left to your own devices to make introductions. Having the initiative to introduce yourself to others can make you appear confident and approachable—two pluses for a first impression.]

---

3. Do you possess good listening skills? Think specifically about whether you can listen to directions once and be able to follow them precisely, whether you "zone out" when someone is talking to you, and whether you can be sympathetic to what is being said when need be. In addition, factor in whether you listen critically (analyzing what you hear) or if you just believe everything you hear.

    My listening skills are:

Excellent   ✳ **Sufficient**   **Need Work**   **Embarrassing**

[If you have to ask for clarifications numerous times because you weren't listening effectively, your perceived competence as a professional person suffers. Also, not believing everything you hear can be a good quality as long as you have sufficient background to ask reasonable questions for clarification. Listen carefully and critically, and ask questions when comments don't make sense.]

---

4. Do you have the skill to receive criticism gracefully and the strength to issue criticism when the job calls for it?

    My communication skills for issuing and receiving criticism are:

Excellent   **Sufficient**   ✳ **Need Work**   **Embarrassing**

[Many people get defensive when someone criticizes their ideas or skills. If you can issue a "Thanks, I'll take that under consideration" and seriously do so, you'll be far better off than people who give a million excuses for why they do what they do. Analyzing criticism thoroughly allows you to improve quickly and remain a valued colleague. The flip side of receiving criticism is giving it to someone else. If that thought makes you somewhat uneasy, you want to remind yourself that the workplace only gets better when people actively evaluate what is going on and perform tasks competently.]

---

5. Do you have strong conversational skills? Think about whether you monopolize verbal time, have balanced conversations, or don't talk at all. Do you keep conversation topics pleasant, or are you always complaining? Do you ask other people about themselves to show interest and to keep the conversation flowing?

   My conversational skills are:

   Excellent   **Sufficient**   **Need Work**   **Embarrassing**

[Being a good conversationalist often makes people pleasant to have in the workplace. Being upbeat, positive, asking questions that show you want to get to know another person while keeping conversations balanced are ways to accomplish this verbal task. People who are always complaining or exuding negative energy are very difficult to work with.]

---

6. Do you think carefully about your own communication and the communication around you? Think specifically about whether you monitor (thinking about what you are saying before you say it and reviewing what you said after you say it) and whether you jump to conclusions without gathering factual information.

   My communication analysis skills are:

   Excellent   **Sufficient**   **Need Work**   **Embarrassing**

[People who monitor their communication figure out what is working, what didn't work, what should be said, and what shouldn't be said. Don't be the kind of person who says the first thought that pops into your mind. Also, get the facts. If you hear a piece of gossip, gather factual information. You can get into a lot of trouble in the workplace by jumping to conclusions and acting on rumors.]

So overall, how do your skills measure up? You can analyze your intrapersonal skills long before you enter the workplace. Conversations and careers are stronger when you approach language as a positive force for personal growth and change. Each of us feels we are good at analyzing the communication issues (verbal/nonverbal) of others, but how often do we think about why we react to others the way we do? You can't always count on another person to communicate effectively, but you can choose to communicate appropriately yourself. We hope the course you are taking will help you to do further analysis of your communication style. This textbook also provides more discussion of some of these skills in upcoming chapters.

FINAL THOUGHTS

Understanding the perceptual process and related perception concepts is critical to becoming an effective communicator. You must understand why you assign meaning the way you do to words, actions, situations, and people, so you can improve your communication style and avoid miscommunication. Once you understand your own perceptions and how the perceptual process works, you'll be better able to analyze why other communicators perceive phenomena and assign meaning the way they do. You should be able to think more critically and clearly about concepts such as stereotyping and attribution as well.

There are fascinating challenges waiting for you as you acclimate to new business situations, perhaps even new regions of the country or world with unique cultures and people. As you work through the perceptual process of organizing and assigning meaning to unfamiliar behaviors and events, you must always be aware of the personal potential for saying or doing the wrong thing. As you gain a more acute awareness of yourself and your ability to communicate effectively with other people, don't jump to conclusions regarding the verbal and nonverbal behavior of others. A simple question can assist you in understanding colleagues; seeking clarity through perception checking will help you become a more effective communicator.

Do your best to manage your own perceptual process so others consistently see you as a solid, credible communicator and someone they would like to get to know better. Your credibility is anchored by a thorough understanding of who you are, your values, and your ethical decision-making skills. This is why a thorough intrapersonal examination of who you really are is vital to successful communication. Take nothing for granted. Be constantly aware of your own skills and qualities as well as those of others.

KEY TERMS

Communication skills
Interpretation and response
Organization
Perception checking
Perceptual process
Personal qualities (skills)

Selection
Selective attention
Self-assessment
Self-concept
Self-esteem
Values

EXERCISES

1. How do other people perceive your strengths and weaknesses? Ask the opinion of at least five people.

2. What skills do you feel you possess that match an employer's needs? Do these skills target your career area?

3. What computer and electronic communication skills can you offer an employer?

4. Discuss how your two best personal qualities fit with your career interest.

5. What do you value most in life?

Job Searches, Résumés, and Cover Letters

GOALS

After reading this chapter you should be able to:

✓ Identify all relevant experiences for a résumé

✓ Create and design an effective résumé format

✓ Write an effective objective

✓ Select unique language to enhance the résumé

✓ Gather appropriate examples and descriptions for a cover letter

✓ Create and design an appropriate cover letter

✓ List the parts of a cover letter and résumé

✓ Understand the implications of making information public

✓ Analyze your own social networking information and make changes where necessary

Your self-assessment (chapter 2) covered your interests, self-esteem, values, personal qualities, and communication skills. Analyze your assessment carefully as you begin to think about an initial employment position, the various companies who have employment possibilities for your skills and interests, and the areas of the country where you would enjoy living. You should also consider the type of climate you would be the most comfortable living in while not at work: warm/cold; east/west; urban/rural, etc. Knowing where you want to live and the kind of people you want as neighbors and colleagues can assist you in making better decisions about the companies to pursue during a job search. Do not send résumés to potential employers if you have no interest in working for them or living in the region in which they are located. You do not want employers to feel they have wasted their time and money pursuing you just to have you reject them at the last minute. The corporate world is interconnected. You need to be honest and prepared to accept a position if the company offers you one.

A thorough analysis of job titles and employee responsibilities within a company is also necessary when matching your skills to various positions. Companies may use the same titles to describe a position, but the skill base required can be completely different. Without researching a company, you may find yourself applying for a position that sounds promising in an ad but for which you do not possess the necessary skills. Such a situation is quite embarrassing during a job interview, and you can avoid this embarrassment with a thorough website search and/or an informative phone interview with someone in human resources or another individual within the company. The goal of the preliminary job investigation is to appear as professionally prepared as possible. This research task takes initiative on your part, but it can also pay off as you apply for a position that suits your abilities rather than one that is totally wrong for your skills and values.

Once you have identified where you want to live and the responsibilities you'd like to assume, and you've researched the ad and company, your next task in your career search is preparing a résumé. As you think about what to include on a résumé, it is useful to ask family members, friends, and former employers to share their thoughts with you about your greatest assets. Listen to the information people share without reacting to any of their views or suggestions. This is not a time to argue or get defensive—it is a time to gather information. Once you talk to other people about your strongest assets and values, you can analyze their statements and compare this list of perceptions to your self-assessment. Every point of comparison that matches your written document gives you a better idea of a "selling point" to mention in the wording on your résumé.

Wendy Enelow and Louise Kursmark (2010) offer some suggestions when deciding what to include in your résumé or cover letter. If you are graduating from college and do not have much work experience, highlight professional skills you developed while working on team projects at school. Look at your academic experiences for leadership skills, which are important in a work environment and illustrate your potential. Highlight academic achievements, which indicate both your intelligence and competitiveness. Most importantly, be sure to connect your skills, experience, and interests to what the employer needs. Communicate that you understand business priorities and are ready to contribute to the success of the company.

With this employment research and skills research behind you, you can now begin writing your résumé.

RÉSUMÉS

A **résumé** is a document that reflects your skills, knowledge, and work history. You send it to potential employers, and they determine, based on how you present yourself on this single sheet of paper, whether they are interested in further contact with you concerning employment. You should choose descriptive words carefully and include information that makes the reader want to meet you. Since the résumé leads to an interview and employment, it is extremely important to present yourself effectively and accurately.

ETHICAL ENCOUNTERS

You decide to list an academic discipline as a minor area of study even though you did not take all of the required courses to qualify for an official minor designation on your transcript. Is this decision a good one?

Most employers only spend about ten seconds glancing at your résumé. Imagine trying to read a stack of 60, 150, or over 1,000 résumés to fill one opening in a company. The task is daunting. In order to whittle a pile of applicants down to a manageable size, employers look through the stack of résumés very quickly to see if they can initially eliminate any candidates who do not fit the posted job requirements.

Think of this as an altered corporate version of the cliché "your life flashes before their eyes." In this case, your life is in print. A résumé immediately goes into the discard pile if it is not visually attractive, easy to read, or relevant for the position.

Résumé Sections

So where do you start? The first thing to do is to gather all of the information about your school, work, and volunteer experience as well as any special skills you have or projects you completed. There are a variety of sections you might include on your résumé. Some of the things you might include are:

- Objective

- Employment history

- Specific skills you have that are unique (everyone knows how to use Microsoft Word at this point, so that is not worth listing, but if you know a specific software application, you may want to include it)

- Foreign language fluency

- Community service

- Honors and awards

- Organizational memberships

- Leadership opportunities

- References (if you choose to include them)

These sections are self-explanatory with the exception of objectives and references. If you review articles on résumé writing and interviewing, you will find about 60 percent of sources recommend using an objective whereas 40 percent do not. In making your decision about whether to use an objective, you should consult with professionals in your field. If you do decide an objective is important, you must keep in mind that this statement is the very first item on the résumé and makes your first impression. You must write a brilliant objective that resonates with potential employers, or you will end up in the discard pile. Everyone knows your objective is to get a job. Don't state the obvious. You must highlight your abilities with solid writing in the objective.

Strong, targeted objectives generally use a format that highlights the applicant's strongest skills (The Right Job, n.d.); for example:

Objective: An xxx position in an organization where yyy and zzz would be needed.

Xxx is the name of the position you seek. Yyy and zzz are the most compelling personal qualities, abilities, or achievements that will really make you stand out from the other applicants. The research you have previously done to find out what is most important to the employer will provide you with the information to fill in yyy and zzz. For example:

Objective: A software sales position in an organization where a consistent record of generating new accounts, exceeding sales targets, and enthusiastic customer relations is needed.

The objective is your attention-getting device; it immediately showcases your best skills. When written well, the objective captures the attention of the employer and invites further exploration of the résumé. Consider the difference between the two objectives below.

Ineffective: To get a video-editing position.

Effective: To obtain a video-editing position in a company where enthusiasm, technical skill, and self-motivation are desired.

The effective objective would be a great persuasive statement at the top of the résumé.

Think about your references as well. Some professions expect you to add the line "References Available Upon Request." Others expect your references (name, title, company, contact information) to be there. You need to let every reference, and/or employer, you list on your résumé know that you mentioned them so they remember who you are and what you did. This professional courtesy guarantees that they can talk intelligently about you with human resources personnel when a prospective employer contacts them to discuss your job performance.

Language of the Résumé

Once you have gathered the information, you write each of the sections for the résumé. The language you use needs to be concise, exciting, and descriptive. Tech Directions (2004) also advises that the language of a résumé must be truthful.

- Do not tell a lie or mistruth.
- Do not include any negative information. (p.27)

All of the résumé's information can be checked by human resources personnel or an interviewer prior to contacting you as well as after they have spoken to you. For example, various organizations require a community service component of all employees. It may be tempting to list your community service activity on your résumé without mentioning that it was mandatory, but this is not a wise decision. If an interviewer checks with the head of the volunteer organization to find out what you actually did and they can't remember your name, the interviewer knows you have exaggerated this work claim and will assume other material on your résumé is suspect to exaggeration also. This fact usually eliminates you from job consideration. The volunteer project might look better on the résumé by describing the skills acquired during the work effort rather than simply mentioning the name of the organization. It is important to find unique words to describe yourself but not at the expense of truthfulness.

Exaggerating your actual accomplishments to get the reader's attention is not only unethical, it can cost you your credibility and your position should you be hired. Employers may review your résumé even after you work in a company as they consider you for advancement. A misstatement on your résumé that wasn't questioned during initial employment can catch up with you at this phase of your career.

Today's employment marketplace is fluid and volatile. Corporate restructuring leads to downsizing, and industries are now looking for new ways to survive with fewer employees and more technology. They want an employee who can make money for the company; therefore, it is useful to look at yourself and your skills in a professional way as you select the appropriate words to express your accomplishments on paper. What are you really good at doing? Does your work and volunteer history demonstrate this passion and talent? Words need to reflect your passion to enable someone who reads your résumé to see immediately what you are capable of doing. In addition, a reader should have an idea of what to expect when you walk into his or her office for an interview.

Examine the sections of your résumé for exciting language. Tech Directions (2004) states, "Use active verbs, not passive. Start each statement with a verb" (p. 26). You should never use the word "I" in the résumé either. "Designed and created flyers" is more active and exciting than "I made flyers."

In addition, Mara Woloshin (2009, p. 7) suggests an editing technique for cover letters that can put you above the rest of the crowd: "When proofreading, modify your modifiers from insecure thinking terms (I feel, I believe, I hope), to active action terms (I am committed, I am confident that)."

Taking the extra time to really look at each word you have selected and to make active and exciting adjustments can elevate your résumé over those of the rest of the people seeking the same job.

Formatting and Layout

Once you have gathered the information and written each of the sections, you need to figure out what kind of format you want to use. There are multiple templates available; but because many people use them, you may look like everyone else applying for the job. Sometimes, a unique format can set you apart.

The essential list for résumé construction includes:

- Be visually attractive

- No typos or errors of any kind

- Showcase your qualities, strengths, and experience

- Show specific instances where you've done what you say you can do

- Follow the format required by your professional area

Additionally, certain résumé requirements vary from person to person and/or from profession to profession, so you'll need to make decisions concerning:

- Whether to limit the résumé to one page

- Whether to use a paper color other than white

- Whether to use multiple fonts

- Whether to use graphics

- Whether to use a personal picture (typically only for actors and models)

Page limitations are another area where you need to check résumé standards in your field. At one time, résumés were only one page in length. That is still true in some fields. One of our former students wanted to work on Capitol Hill. She sent out 100 copies of a two-page résumé. She was bewildered when she did not get a single inquiry. After doing more research, she found that the norm on Capitol Hill, in her field, was a one-page résumé. Apparently, anything over one page went into the trash immediately. She retooled her résumé to one page and received a number of interviews. A two-page or longer résumé may be perfectly acceptable in certain fields. In these professions, you would not want to limit yourself to only one page if you had enough relevant information to include—but be certain that everything you list is, in fact, relevant to the position for which you want an interview.

Once you have all of the text together, think about its formatting. Julie Allen, a human resources specialist, skims through multiple résumés a week. A potential candidate has about 30 seconds to capture her attention. Allen highlights presentation as one important area and emphasizes that the résumé should be concise yet compelling.

Presentation.   Your résumé should look professional, which does not necessarily mean fancy fonts, graphics, or a lot of bells and whistles. If you are sending a résumé via e-mail or replying via a website, the original formatting may be lost. If you have the option of attaching the document, send it as a pdf file, which will retain the formatting. A pdf file isn't easily altered, which makes it a wise choice.

- Use standard margins.
- Single space between items, and double space between sections.
- Highlight items using boldface rather than changing fonts. Items that you want to stand out can be bolded such as your name, employer's name, or the name of the institution.
- Use bullets to highlight accomplishments. Keep bulleted items to one or two lines. Bullets make a résumé look clean, clear, and crisp.

Additional Résumé Strategies

Even if your word choice and layout are intriguing, you can sabotage that positive impression immediately if there are typos in your résumé. Tech Directions (2004) advises, "Have someone else proofread your résumé—don't rely on a computer's spell-checker program" (p. 26). Someone else may see things that you missed.

As you craft your résumé, it is helpful to cross-reference its claims with the information you've created on social networking sites. The social perceptions you share on the web need to match the perceptions you create with your résumé. A potential employer may check your site (see discussion in a following section).

Tech Directions (2004, p. 26) suggests another excellent strategy: "In addition to mailing your résumé, e-mail it as well, and always bring several extra copies when applying for a job in person." You look extremely competent if the interviewer cannot find your résumé, and you are able to hand them a fresh copy. And honestly, by the time you read this book, you may not be sending a résumé at all. Most companies are shifting to online applications; however, most such programs have a place to attach a formatted résumé.

Placing yourself on the job market is an excellent time to review the professional nature of the e-mail address on your résumé as well as the message on your voice mail. These two items can make a good impression on a stranger when they see/hear them while considering you for a position with their company. You should clearly shape your e-mail address to reveal that you are prepared for a career (not hotvanilla-chick.com or gasgiant.com). Your phone message should be polished and articulate, with no background distractions like funky music recorded at a high level so it's difficult to hear what you are saying. We recommend that you update both of these items for professionalism prior to sending out the first résumé. In addition, you should also reexamine your social media sites through the eye of a professional outsider who is trying to evaluate you for career possibilities.

You also want to think about ways to make your résumé look unique and stand out, but without compromising professional quality. For example, we had a student who tried to make her résumé look unique by incorporating heart-shaped bullets. While we admired her creativity, it was a little too "cutesy" for corporate America.

Many large companies scan résumés and store the files on a computer. This means no human being looks at your résumé initially. Instead, a computer searches a résumé for key words. Therefore, it is important to use the key words of your profession when describing your work history. Some people place a list of keywords at the bottom of their résumés, but once a human being looks at the résumé and notices the trick, they may have an unfavorable reaction and discard the résumé. In addition, fancy formatting and marbled papers do not scan well. Those choices would put you immediately into the discard pile. If the company requires electronic submission, in some cases, the text of your résumé must be left justified, with no formatting. Most company websites explain their review process and formatting requirements for résumé submissions.

So let's look at a sample résumé to see how one person chose to present herself for employment:

HOLLY K. BAKER

1010 Bennington Dr. ~ Orlando, FL 32801 ~ 555.123.4567 ~ bakerhk@msn.com

OBJECTIVE

A media relations position in a company where a creative and reliable public relations graduate with experience in campaign development and superior interpersonal and written communication skills would be valued.

SKILLS SUMMARY

- Led students and assisted marketing manager in the planning and implementation of a public relations campaign and special event for a local, nonprofit organization
- Constructed personal and small business websites using Microsoft Expression Web and assisted in directing Microsoft Expression Web training session
- Proficient in Microsoft Word, Excel, Power Point, Publisher, Web Expressions, HTML and currently learning Adobe software
- Ability to create press kits and compose press releases, fact sheets, news articles, and speeches
- Well-organized, detail-oriented, and energetic with abilities to prioritize, multitask, and rapidly learn new procedures and computer applications
- Proven aptitude for maintaining strong consumer and vendor relationships

EDUCATION

Corning Community College, Corning, NY
Associate of Science in Liberal Arts; General Studies, May 2007, GPA: 3.96
Mansfield University, Mansfield, PA
Bachelor of Science in Mass Communication; Public Relations, May 2009, GPA: 3.78

[handwritten note in margin: Switch]

PROFESSIONAL EXPERIENCE

Member Service Representative   Corning, NY
Corning Community YMCA   09/02–07/05, 04/06–present

- Assisted senior director by proofreading YMCA newsletters, brochures, and additional communication materials as well as screening calls and recording and delivering messages for staff directors
- Communicated YMCA policies and services to members, responded to member questions and concerns, promoted membership and program sales to visitors, and conducted facility tours
- Responsible for membership and program registrations, daily accounting, maintaining accuracy of electronic database, determining scholarship membership eligibility, and opening/closing facility

Innkeeper Assistant   Hector, NY
Seneca Springs Resort   05/09–10/09

- Contributed written material for company website and designed guest entertainment packages and print communication materials including inventory forms, memos, fact sheets, and event invitations

- Assisted in developing company marketing strategies and planning resort events, researched vendor products and prices, and visited regional businesses to discuss participation in resort events
- Greeted and escorted resort guests, replied to e-mail/phone inquiries, managed staff schedule, assisted in payroll accounting, and organized hard copy files

Writing Center Peer Tutor   Corning, NY
Corning Community College   08/04–05/05, 08/06–05/07

- Directed private sessions with students to help improve critical reading, professional writing, research and word processor skills
- Edited and proofread student compositions
- Conducted seminars endorsing the benefits of using the Writing Center, organized student files, maintained order of small library, restocked educational literature and print supplies

Guest Services Representative   Elmira, NY
Econo Lodge   06/06-08/06

- Replied to e-mail/phone inquiries, negotiated reservation rates, completed reservations, collected and accounted daily income, and responded to guest needs

Bookseller   Ocoee, FL
Waldenbooks   08/05–01/06

- Greeted and assisted customers, managed seasonal calendar kiosk, stocked merchandise, and designed store displays

HONORS, AWARDS AND PUBLICATIONS

- President's List of Distinguished Undergraduate Scholars, Fall 2008, Spring 2009
- Phi Theta Kappa member, with distinction, 2007
- Corning Community College Award for Excellence in Communication Studies, 2007
- SCOP First Place Fiction Award, 2004 and SCOP Cover Art Design, 2004 and 2007
- Baker, H. (2008, Dec. 11). Think Green. *Corning Family YMCA 2009 Winter/Spring Brochure*, p. 16.
- Baker, H. (2008, Dec. 11). What Parents Should Know about Childhood Obesity. *Corning Family YMCA 2009 Winter/Spring Brochure*, p. 10.
- Baker, H. (2008, Oct. 27). Life in a College Town: Lessons about Time. *Williamsport Sun-Gazette*, p. B-1.
- Baker, H. (2008, Nov. 20). Prepare Yourself for a Pennsylvania Winter. *Flashlight*, p. 9.

REFERENCES

Nancy Richards, *Senior Director*
Corning Community YMCA, 127 Centerway, Corning, NY 14830
678-901-2345, nancy@someplace.org

Dr. Jane Jones, *Full Professor of Communication & Theater*
Mansfield University, 212 Spruce Manor, Mansfield, PA 16933
012-345-6789, jjones@anotherplace.com

Lucy Foster, *Innkeeper*
Seneca Springs Resort, Route 414, Hector, NY 14840
123-456-7890, foster@athirdplace.com

Although an employer may have received your résumé online, you should still carry hard copies to the interview so you can leave a copy with various individuals you meet on-site. Some of these people have not seen your résumé in advance, and a paper copy gives them a chance to scan the material as they converse with you. In addition, they can scan your résumé in detail after you leave if you've made a strong impression on them.

COVER LETTERS

Now that you've written your résumé, you need to write an appealing cover letter to accompany it. A **cover letter** allows you to convince an employer that you possess the experience and skills to fill a specific advertised position. Every job description lists the requirements they are looking for when they consider you for a position. Since the résumé lists your best skills and experiences, the cover letter gives you the opportunity to target the advertisement itself. Your letter needs to address each posted skill for employment consideration. Therefore, you write a new cover letter to match the requirements of every job for which you apply, since the cover letter will address the specifics of a posted position.

Typically the cover letter highlights the portions of your résumé that reinforce the various skills an employer is looking for. Some employers read cover letters first, and if they are impressed by what they read, they'll consult your résumé for more information. Other employers use computers to scan your résumé. If you possess the basic qualifications for the position, the employer will read your cover letter to see how you sell yourself in fully developed sentences. Make sure to use well-worded phrases and well-structured sentences to showcase the specific skills/experiences on your résumé that match the advertisement. Your cover letter should be concise, creative, and direct.

ETHICAL ENCOUNTERS

You spot an online ad describing a position that would be perfect for you. You immediately contact a friend to write a cover letter for you because you know her writing style is superior to your own. The friend agrees to write the letter, and you quickly forward the letter and your résumé to the web address listed. The company contacts you to do an initial Skype interview. During the interview, the interviewer compliments you on the way you wrote the cover letter. How do you respond to the compliment?

The cover letter is normally less than one page in length and follows a basic structure. Begin with a greeting such as "To Whom It May Concern" if the specific name of a human resource contact isn't listed in the advertisement. The first paragraph typically indicates that you are writing to apply for X job that you found in Y publication/website/etc. Indicating where you found the position listed allows companies to keep a tally of where their advertising dollars are obtaining the best results for new employees. The final sentence of this paragraph should be a concise statement about what you can offer the company.

The second paragraph should persuasively match your qualifications to the job itself. This is the "key" paragraph in your letter, since it shows an employer that you've actually read the company's ad and have the specific skills required. Be engaging in telling your story and allowing a little of your personality to come through as you describe why you are an exact match for the job.

Make sure that you focus your comments on the position advertised as you write the body of your letter. Stephen Rushmore (2009, p. 18) explains that one of the biggest problems with cover letters is that "the applicant is interested in too many areas and shows no focus, unique expertise or experience." Focus on a couple of areas that demonstrate the qualities the ad is asking for. Use specifics in describing your ability to do what the employer needs.

The final paragraph should thank an employer for taking the time to read your application. Some people advise specifying a time when you will follow up, but our feeling is that such a statement could be perceived as presumptuous. A simple "I look forward to hearing from you" should be effective. However, Rushmore (2009, p. 19) states that the best ending line in a cover letter he received was: "If you give me a chance I will not disappoint you and you will not regret hiring me." What do you think?

Many companies talk about their application and follow-up procedures in the job ad itself or on their corporate website (another reason for you not to risk a negative impression by stating when you will follow up). Web-generated job ads usually tell you that the company received your material. Some companies send postcards when they receive your material, and others do not notify you at all. The company knows you want a job, and that's why you are sending them your material, so don't state the obvious. Make the final paragraph concise and to-the-point, as a professional person would do.

Close with "sincerely" or "respectfully" and your typed name, but don't forget to sign the cover letter above your typed name. Your typed name must match the name printed on your résumé (middle name, middle initial, etc.). A pen with black ink is the best to use when signing your name because people can read it easily if the employer photocopies your cover letter for internal distribution. It doesn't hurt to make sure your black pen works on scrap paper before you begin to sign the cover letter. Going back over the signature a few times doesn't make a professional impression. If your pen fails, you need to print a new copy of the cover letter and sign it to send with your résumé.

In addition, we recommend that you use the same graphic header for your cover letter that you design for your résumé. Consistent design and paper texture ties the cover letter and résumé together as a professional package. It is also useful to an employer should your materials become separated.

The cover letter and résumé open the door to a job that interests you. Once they are sent, you wait for a positive response and the scheduling of an interview. The following is an example of an advertised position and the cover letter it elicited.

Media Relations/Public Relations Professional

✓ **About the Job**

This position is responsible for leading our local/regional media relations and public relations efforts, increasing public and brand awareness.

Media Relations: Primary duties include writing press releases, pitching to media, managing press coverage/clips and implementing PR campaigns. Liaisons with managers, administrators, reporters and other external parties. Research and write releases, fact sheets, news pitches, bylined articles, position papers, op-eds, press kits, background information, talking points, and other press materials. This position will support increasing press activity — including proactive media outreach and pitches. Identifies and prepares spokespersons for interviews. Maintains company newsroom page.

Public Relations: Supports company PR activities and events. This position will cultivate relationships internally and externally — to include our local media.

Social Media: Leverages social networks to communicate messages and build relationships with internal and external parties — including the media. Contributes parallel media/social media content/posts for publication.

✓ **Position Requirements**

Background: Seeking seasoned professional with 3–5 years related experience in media relations and public relations within a fast-paced business environment, with the ability to multitask. Must be media savvy, connected to current industry news events and a self-starter. Creative mind with a track record of generating and implementing new ideas and story angles. Excellent media, PR, writing, proof-reading, editing, and pitching skills required. Must be proficient in MS Office products with a high level of proficiency in MS Word.

Education: Minimum 4-year degree in Mass Communications, Marketing or related field.

Other Skills: Public relations and Web/new media experience preferred. Ability to research, read, comprehend, and write complex communications. Ability to effectively present information in large and small group environments. Must have excellent communication and interpersonal skills. Analytical skills, Excel and Power Point proficiency a plus. Must have demonstrated multitasking skills and be able to work both independently and with a group.

Here is the letter that Holly writes to accompany her résumé:

HOLLY K. BAKER

1010 Bennington Dr. ~ Orlando, FL 32801 ~ 555.123.4567 ~ bakerhk@msn.com

---

April 15, 2012

Mr. John James
Human Resources
NRT-Southeast Region
1400 Sunshine St.
Sarasota, FL 34230

Dear Mr. James,

In response to the listing on monster.com for a Media Relations/Public Relations Professional at NRT, I am submitting my résumé for consideration for the opportunity. After reviewing the requirements of and qualifications for this position, I am confident that my education in public relations and professional experience in consumer services and marketing development make me a competitive candidate for this opportunity.

I am an organized, creative, self-motivated, and enthusiastic professional with exceptional verbal and written communication abilities as well as excellent multitasking, time-management, and web-design skills. I possess a Bachelor of Science degree in Mass Communication, Public Relations from Mansfield University in Mansfield, Pennsylvania, and have assisted in the design and execution of a public relations campaign and special event. My professional positions as a member services representative and administrative assistant at a resort have given me seven years experience in composing communication pieces, positively representing and promoting businesses, planning events, and maintaining valuable relationships with consumers and vendors.

I am sincerely interested in discussing how my experience and skills may benefit NRT. Thank you for your time and consideration.

Respectfully,

Holly K. Baker   (Holly's signature in black ink)

Holly K. Baker

What are the strengths and weaknesses of Holly's letter? What would you do differently to make her stand out even more? Thinking about the changes you would make in Holly's cover letter is a good reminder of how writing styles vary from one person to another. The true judge of your written style is the person who reads your material, so spend some time proofing your letter to make sure it's the best it can be. A cover letter allows you to demonstrate your written abilities quite clearly to a potential employer.

SOCIAL NETWORKING, REFERENCES, AND JOB SEARCHING

Once you have created an exciting résumé and cover letter, a potential employer is ready to examine it. But be prepared for scrutiny of the material you place on your résumé and cover letter. Eve Tahmincioglu, an MSNBC.com contributor, writes about important considerations for references.

- Think very carefully about people listed on your social networking sites. More hiring managers use these sites for information about job candidates, so your contacts should be people you trust who will give you a good recommendation. Use the privacy settings if you don't want a potential employer to see your connections.

- Call your references ahead of time and make sure they know what type of job you're applying for. Make sure they are aware of why you left your last job so their account matches what you have said. Alert your references to be prepared with facts.

- Ask your references not to exaggerate your qualifications; too much overstatement could raise red flags.

- If a hiring manager tells you he is going to contact a former boss or subordinate who does not appear on your reference list and you know that person is likely to give you a bad review, be honest. You might say something like, "I don't mind you calling Mary, but don't be surprised if she doesn't give you a glowing report. We just didn't hit it off." (Resist bad-mouthing anyone.)

Tahmincioglu writes that managers may be reluctant to give recommendations because they fear litigation from former employees if the comments are not positive. In turn, many employees omit employers from their résumés if the comments are likely to be negative. Hiring managers are aware of both problems and use social networking sites such as LinkedIn and Facebook to find information. Some firms ask job candidates to sign waivers promising not to sue former employers if the reviews are negative.

Online screening of social networking sites is becoming more prevalent in the hiring process with the technically advanced generation. Managing the images and information on your social networking sites is not only good personal marketing; it establishes your professional credibility instantly when used as a background check for the facts listed on your résumé.

"Social networking is a great way to make connections with potential job opportunities and promote your personal brand across the Internet," said Rosemary Haefner (2009), Vice President of Human Resources at CareerBuilder. "Make sure you are using this resource to your advantage by conveying a professional image and underscoring your qualifications."

Haefner recommends the following DOs and DON'Ts to maintain a positive online image:

1. DO clean up digital dirt BEFORE you begin your job search. Remove any photos, content, and links that can work against you in an employer's eyes. [Your authors suggest that while you are in college, don't put compromising information on social networking sites.]

2. DO consider creating your own professional group on sites like Facebook or BrightFuse.com to establish relationships with thought leaders, recruiters, and potential referrals.

3. DO keep gripes offline. Keep the content focused on the positive, whether that relates to professional or personal information. Make sure to highlight specific accomplishments inside and outside of work.

4. DON'T forget others can see your friends, so be selective about who you accept as friends. Monitor comments made by others. Consider using the "block comments" feature or setting your profile to "private" so only designated friends can view it.

5. DON'T mention your job search if you're still employed.

Social networking encourages freedom of expression, but when a corporation accesses an individual's personal information to determine if someone is a good fit for the company, when does an employer's quest to determine your worth to the company become a violation of your right to privacy?

Germany is the first country to draft privacy legislation protecting potential employees as well as employees from eavesdropping employers. They are considering legislation to make it illegal for companies to check your Facebook and other social networking sites for personal information about you.

Although a potential employee may never be able to prove a position was lost due to digital surveillance, this legal discussion in Germany is another reason to think about your digital footprint throughout your working life.

Adapted from http://www.nytimes.com/2010/08/26/business/global/26fbook.html

If your written persuasion effectively entices an employer to contact you, you need to think about one more piece of personal organization prior to a potential phone call—how you answer the phone! If the contact number you provide to prospective employers is a landline shared with family members or roommates, remind them that an employer might be calling so they answer the phone appropriately. You might consider leaving a list of the companies you have contacted next to the phone to remind yourself and others of the contacts you've initiated. This idea may sound a little formal, but the professional tone you set with a corporate person trying to reach you is worth the effort.

If your contact number is your personal cell phone, you need to be alert and ready to communicate *every* time it rings. Try to imagine the reaction of a human resource staff member when you answer the phone on a busy day and say, "Who?" because you have no idea what companies you contacted with résumés. This is not the way to get a job or make a good first impression. When you place yourself on the job market, your future is on the line each time the phone rings, and you need to answer it professionally. If your initial written and mental preparation goes well, you will receive an invitation to continue the interview process through a phone or e-mail request to meet you.

You occasionally may be interviewed for jobs that don't exist. Human resource personnel are always looking for potential employees and a good interview can place you in a file entitled "future hires." It is also possible to interview for an advertised position already reserved for an internal candidate. The interviewers know the person within the organization and he/she possesses an obvious advantage for a position over an "outsider." Sometimes, this happens for legal reasons. They know who they want in the job, but they are legally required to interview a certain number of candidates. Your efforts may be in vain. Then again, an interview can mean employment if you present yourself in an exceptional manner.

FINAL THOUGHTS

Creating a compelling résumé can be a daunting task. One suggestion to make the written process easier is to treat the layout of your information as a board game. Type your name, address, jobs, skills, education, and so forth onto a piece of paper and cut the information into separate strips. Then, begin to move them around on top of a full sheet of paper until you like the arrangement and order of the material. Now, you are ready to type all of your material into an initial document for final review and editing prior to printing. You might eventually move the education category listed at the top of your résumé to the bottom as your work experience eventually replaces the initial importance of possessing a high school diploma or college degree. Similarly, some work experience will also disappear from your résumé over time since your most recent employment and skills are what an employer wants to see.

Each cover letter you write is different from the one before it because you write a cover letter to target the specific job you are seeking. You should pull various skills and/or responsibilities from your résumé to feature in every cover letter you write. You shape the letter's information to a position's requirements. Although you write the cover letter creatively, the information you feature is always factual and truthful. The format of a cover letter is just like a good public speech: introduction, body (why your experience/skills meet the requirements of the position), and conclusion. A solid cover letter takes practice but your writing improves each time you apply for an employment opportunity.

A cover letter and résumé are the most important pieces of persuasive writing you do upon leaving school. They need to capture the attention and interest of professional people in the business world. Once they have accomplished that goal and you are contacted for an in-person, phone, or Skype interview, your oral communication skills and interpersonal skills are the ones that open the door to a career. The interview tells the corporation if you fit into its culture and possess the character and skills required to be productive.

KEY TERMS

Cover Letter   Résumé

EXERCISES

1. Write your résumé. Use the appropriate format and language of your career discipline.

2. Write a cover letter for two job ads. Attach a copy of the ad to each letter for submission.

3. Research the company of your dreams and analyze the skills necessary to work there. This research also applies to graduate school in case that is the next step.

4

Interviewing

GOALS

After reading this chapter you should be able to:

✓ Understand the preparation that is necessary for an interview

✓ Analyze your interview clothing to make the best impression

✓ Define behavioral interviewing

✓ Prepare and practice behavioral interview answers

✓ Define a brainteaser

✓ Compare and contrast phone, Skype, and stress interviews

✓ Understand the implications of communicating effectively after the interview

Interviewing is a process where you demonstrate effective communication skills to obtain employment or promotion. Interviewing involves perhaps the most important persuasion in which you will engage after graduation, or if your employment is terminated by corporate restructuring, or if you decide to change jobs. Without a persuasive résumé and cover letter, you will not obtain an interview opportunity. Many job applicants who appear terrific on paper don't make a solid first impression during the in-person interview. Your verbal/nonverbal and written skills must complement one another for a successful interview process.

There is no single, perfect communication technique that will impress everyone during an interview. Effective résumé writing and interviewing preparation will vary from profession to profession. Therefore, along with the general tips we provide, we strongly recommend you do a thorough Internet search for interviewing tips within your field. Even with countless "how-to" guides, your success in gaining employment will depend on such key components as your personality, appearance, and work experience. A knowledgeable faculty advisor or professional mentor is a valuable resource when preparing for an interview.

Once your résumé and cover letter attract an employer's attention, an interview opportunity usually follows. You must diligently prepare for the interview. Some individuals think they can simply talk and be themselves. This casual attitude may be your downfall. Employers prefer concise, logical answers to their questions, especially in an era of intense competition for employment.

To be effective in an interview, you must:

- Spend time preparing for the interview
- Be prepared for phone interviews
- Be prepared for Skype interviews
- Be prepared for stress interviews
- Make a great first impression
- Be able to answer questions effectively
- Communicate effectively after the interview

PREPARING FOR AN INTERVIEW

Once you receive an interview confirmation, there are a number of things you can do to plan for a successful, prompt arrival. Make sure you have the proper business address and directions for exactly where you need to go once you locate the building. If the business is a long distance from your location, or in a congested place, use a GPS system to guide you or use Google Maps, MapQuest, or a street map for directions. You should plan where you are going to park your car as well. Remember to take the phone number of your contact along in case you have an unusual complication. Don't hesitate to ask travel questions of your contact person at the organization when you have the initial conversation via e-mail or phone. It is much better to research the trip exhaustively than to get lost.

Another question to ask the contact person is whether you will be interviewing with an individual or a group. Ask for the name(s) of the people with whom you will be interviewing. If possible, look for the individual(s) on the company website ahead of time. This will give you a familiarity with how they look and possibly provide information about their titles and responsibilities. It is useful to remember that names don't always reveal a person's gender. There are a few first names shared equally between men and women. You don't want to look shocked when you meet a woman after mistakenly assuming you would be interviewing with a man.

Research the company well so you know all of its basic information: size of the organization, product(s), scope (local, regional, national, global), number of employees, mission, etc. For example, we once had a job applicant who arrived for a faculty interview and asked how many students were enrolled at our institution. That immediately told us the person had not done any preparation for the interview. Some of the questions you ask an interviewer should evolve from your personal research about the company and its product. Your questions reveal your areas of interest, intuition, intellect, and ability to think on your feet in addition to your interest in the company.

If it has been a few days or weeks since the original appointment was scheduled, it is a good idea to phone or e-mail your contact a day before the scheduled interview to confirm the details of your appointment. Being flexible and adapting to change is important; sometimes despite thorough preparation, you will be surprised when you arrive for an appointment. Corporate or personal emergencies arise and you may be asked to come back another day, or you may be assigned to another person who will conduct the interview. In both cases, a calm, professional response to the situation demonstrates your adaptability instantly. If you are prepared for this difficult and frustrating situation, you have a chance to exhibit a skill useful to the potential employer—adaptability.

Employers describe specific programs or skills in a job ad, and you need to match those exact skills with your experience. Heather Huhman (2009), a career expert, reinforces the idea of paying close attention to every requirement in a job ad: "Be prepared to use the computer in the HR office if specific programs or skills are required in the job ad. Some companies are giving computer problems/quizzes to applicants as part of the interviewing process."

Anything can happen during a job interview, and it is wise to be prepared for the unexpected. A colleague told us about her friend, who had an unusual interview experience. The first question in the interview was would she drive the two of them to lunch. The interviewee was horrified because the condition of her car was less than presentable, with fast-food wrappers and other garbage strewn around the seats and floor. What would the interviewer's perception of the candidate be after that short ride? Although you wouldn't expect an interviewer to see the inside of your car, anything can happen, and you must be prepared. It is just as reasonable to anticipate that an interviewer might walk you to your car after the interview because it's the end of the work day, or the person wants to use the time to ask you a few more questions.

Even if your self-confidence is not high, you'll want to demonstrate competence and assurance. Selena Dehne (2010), a publicist, offers some tips on self-confidence. She encourages you to think about the positive aspects of yourself and don't dwell on negatives or insecurities. Use positive affirmations on a daily basis as you are job hunting and surround yourself with supportive people as you move through the difficult task of seeking employment.

Finally, remember that you are "on" the entire time you are present at the interview site. From the moment you step out of your car, people may be watching you from windows. The same scenario is true with your departure. Until you are safely out of sight, you should appear to be a responsible, professional potential employee. You can collapse later.

TYPES OF INTERVIEWS

It used to be that the only kind of interview you would encounter would be a face-to-face interview on site at a company. Today, interviewers can screen candidates via a phone or Skype interview before going to the expense of an on-site interview. Additionally, within certain fields, applicants need to be prepared for a stress interview.

Phone Interviews

Phone interviews add an interesting dimension to the interview process. This is a good news/bad news situation. The good news is you don't have to worry about your attire or posture. You can use interview notes with answers to potential questions and lists of skills or qualities that you don't want to forget. The bad news is your vocal technique, vocabulary, and verbal style are all overemphasized. Your paralanguage (the vocal techniques you use to emphasize and give meaning to words) is even more important on the phone. Because the listener has no visual cues, your "ums/uhs," pitch, tone of voice, and rate are the focus of the conversation. Speaking too quickly makes you sound nervous. Too many "ums/uhs" make you sound unsure of yourself. Practice conversationally answering questions before you have your phone interview. Concentrate on your grammar and expressing yourself in a concise manner. Stand up while you talk during a phone interview so you have the best breath support for energy and vocal quality. You can tape your notes and résumé on the wall. Also remember you will have no nonverbal feedback in a phone interview. You cannot tell whether the interviewer is smiling and nodding or looking disgusted. Imagine a positive, friendly face on the interviewer to help yourself remain calm.

Skype Interviews

Technology is bringing a new dimension to corporate screening, interviewing, and hiring. For cost-saving reasons as well as speed in filling a vacancy, employers are now conducting interviews via computers using a software application called **Skype** that allows users to make voice calls over the Internet. The computer's camera lens allows the interviewer to see you as well as hear you. They can compare your facial expressions to the enthusiasm in your voice to check your perceived personality and character. You are seen from the waist up or even tighter depending on your distance from the camera. It is important to remember in the Skype interview to look directly into the camera lens to keep your face open to the interviewer. Unlike the telephone interview, you will be able to see the face of the person speaking with you. The camera allows the conversation to be quite similar to face-to-face interpersonal communication.

Skype interviews have advantages and some drawbacks. One interviewer mentioned that a candidate in a Skype interview consistently leaned forward (Kiviat, 2009). While this nonverbal behavior can communicate interest in a face-to-face interview, in the Skype interview it filled the screen with the candidate's face. In another interview, a dog barked continually in the background, and in another the college dorm room of the candidate had clearly not been cleaned or straightened. Bill McGowan, a media coach in New York, suggests making sure there is no bright light behind you because that will make your face appear dark. Other suggestions include wearing clothes that look good on screen—avoid patterns. For a more relaxed presentation, swivel your chair toward the corner of your computer screen and then turn your head back toward the camera. Sit tall but not at a distance so that the first three buttons on your shirt are visible. If possible, do a test run with a friend so you can check color, sound, and your expressions. Be prepared to send your résumé as an attachment if requested.

The advances in technology improve the speed with which a company can make a decision about hiring. The employer can schedule an interview at any time of day and do so almost immediately—no travel time, housing arrangements, meals, etc. are required. The visual interview via computer may seem awkward to individuals over the age of 50, but to the social-networking generation of Americans, it is a natural progression. The psychological adjustment you need to make during a Skype interview is being able to carry on an extemporaneous discussion through a technical channel rather than sitting in the same space with another person. Also be aware that with the Skype application available on cell phones, you could be expected to interview at anytime and anywhere. Think about the implications for looking your best at all times!

Stress Interviews

Another situation you should be prepared to handle is the stress interview. In a **stress interview**, the employer will test you to your limits. We had an accounting major who went to an interview for a financial-planning position. The interviewer looked at her and said, "OK, Heather, here is a stack of travel brochures. I'll be back in 20 minutes, and I expect you to have a persuasive presentation ready for me concerning where I should go on vacation." He exited the room. When he got back and heard her presentation, he immediately launched into his questions. She was not allowed to use any material twice for her answers to 16 questions. When he asked her what her greatest weakness was, she paused for a brief moment, and he badgered her with, "What's the matter Heather, do you think you are perfect?" In this situation, the employer is trying to see how she will hold up under stress. Although this may seem unfair, a job as a financial planner entails dealing with very unhappy customers when the stock market goes down, and the employer needs to know if the employee can handle the pressure.

Another student who had a degree in broadcasting interviewed for a video-editing position. When the student arrived at the studio, they handed him video clips from a breaking story aired earlier the same day. He had 30 minutes to cut his own version of the story for the station. He received no training or explanation of the company's equipment in the editing suite. He finished creating his version of the story within the time limit. The supervisor thanked him for his time and said the senior producer would contact him after screening the applicant's video. No further questions were asked. The interview was over.

A third example of a stressful interview situation can occur when you are interviewed with other applicants. There are times when all applicants are brought into the same room and asked to answer questions in front of one another. We know of two people who have reported being asked to answer the question, "Why should we hire you instead of the specific person on your left."

Thinking about the three scenarios just described, it is important to find out what the interview norm is in your professional field. Are you likely to run into stress interviews? Make sure you can do what you say you can do on your résumé, because you may be tested. For example, if you state that you are bilingual, it is reasonable to assume that the person interviewing you could conduct the interview in the language listed on your résumé. Any hesitation on your part in performing a task or answering a question may give the interviewer a bad impression. Be prepared and remain as relaxed as possible to handle whatever the interviewer throws at you.

MAKING A GREAT IMPRESSION

After your thorough preparation, you are ready to embark on the actual interview. A **first impression** is extremely important in making an interviewer feel comfortable with you. Think back to chapter 2 on perception. Most people will decide in the first few seconds whether you seem competent, whether they will like you, and whether you are a good fit with their company. The way you look when the interviewer first sees you, the way you move as you enter the room, the first words out of your mouth, and how you shake an interviewer's hand can really help your chances of making a great impression.

You must choose your personal **artifacts** carefully. For example, Aaron walks into an interview with an advertising agency in a crisply pressed, jet-black suit. He has a silver dress shirt and gray silk tie; his shoes are highly polished. His belt is black leather with a silver tip. Aaron's appearance establishes him as a person of potential interest when he introduces himself to the interviewer.

Lee Anne is not aware of how important artifact choices are, however. Although she can afford much more expensive clothing than Aaron, she has made some unwise choices for her interview. She chooses a flowery, casual, wrinkled dress. Her shoes have open toes and heels because it is August. The tattoo around her ankle is visible through her nude-colored pantyhose.

Aaron visually communicates success and confidence. There is nothing in his appearance an interviewer could interpret as objectionable. He sticks to the basic principles of the dress code for an advertising position. He realizes, however, if he were interviewing in a more traditional corporation, he should wear a dark suit, a white shirt rather than silver, and a conservative tie. Lee Anne is clueless regarding the image her clothing projects. A flowery dress is simply too casual. Her visible tattoo gives the employer personal information about her personality that could be interpreted in a negative manner. (It is quite possible that Aaron has a tattoo, but it is covered by his suit and not visible to the interviewer.) The best way to make clothing decisions for an interview is to analyze the company thoroughly and to dress as conservatively as possible.

Attire and overall appearance are essential to your potential success during the interview process. You may not be able to afford expensive, well-tailored clothing or gold and sterling silver jewelry, but you can choose colors and fabrics that make you look good. Employees in many companies have a specific look, and you should try to find out what it is prior to an interview. In certain cases, the dress code is casual, and you may look out of place in a tailored suit. It is best to research the dress code for each company with which you secure an interview and to select a comfortable, appropriate outfit plus accessories.

It's not a bad idea to become comfortable wearing dress clothing while you are still in school. Although the thought of occasionally dressing up for class may seem awkward at first, the ease with which you move, sit, and stand in corporate attire will be enhanced if you have some practice before graduation. If finances are tight, be resourceful. You can build your professional look slowly while in college. Ask for interview attire for holiday and birthday gifts. You can begin accumulating items such as shoes, jewelry, ties, scarves, and belts that work even if you gain or lose a little weight.

Clothes affect initial perceptions of your persona—from the most casual moments of life to the most formal. You should always dress appropriately for whatever event you are attending. While you may believe that green hair and face hardware makes you an individualist, that look is rarely comfortable to others in most corporate settings. A good presentational rule is to dress on a daily basis like individuals who have a job you wish to obtain in the future. The dress code is conservative in most companies. Your initial appearance can make your transition to employment easier or more difficult.

In addition, clothing needs to complement your body type. Here are a few of the fundamental rules for the conservative interviewing process.

DOs
- One earring per ear (no earrings for men)
- Either a necklace or a bracelet
- One ring per hand
- Shined shoes
- Plain, conservative tie (no cartoon characters!)

DON'Ts
- No open-toe or open-heel shoes
- No sleeveless outfits (women), no short-sleeved shirts (men)
- No gaudy or noticeable makeup
- No work boots/sneakers

Once the interviewer sees you, you have made your first impression. But his or her perception of you doesn't stop there. Your handshake will add or detract from the first impression. A firm handshake sends the nonverbal message of confidence—a personal quality desired by most interviewers. Wiping sweaty hands on your pants or fumbling with papers so you can extend your hand for a handshake sends a message of incompetence as well as a lack of professional interpersonal experience.

A study by the Kellogg School of Management at Northwestern University found that standing tall will make you act more in charge and can help you stay ahead of the competition (Grant, 2011). Adam Galinsky, the professor who led the study, advises that standing straight will make you perform better in the interview because you will answer with more authority and more confidence. Galinsky refers to postures that make us feel more in charge as "expansive postures." These include sitting with your legs slightly apart or your arm over the back of a chair. However, he also notes that some of the postures are not appropriate for an interview or an office meeting. In those situations, he suggests focusing on sitting upright, expanding your chest, and holding your arms in a relaxed, comfortable position. Joe Navarro, an expert in nonverbal communication for the FBI, emphasizes good eye contact but also cautions not to look around the room as though you own the space. He also suggests leaning forward occasionally to convey enthusiasm; leaning back has the opposite effect.

Katie Lorenz of CareerBuilder.com uses "soft skills" in assisting her to make a decision about an employee:

> Each company looks for a different mix of skills and experience depending on the business it's in. Yet it's no longer enough to be a functional expert. To complement these unique core competencies, there are certain "soft skills" every company looks for in a potential hire.
>
> "Soft skills" refer to a cluster of personal qualities, habits, attitudes and social graces that make someone a good employee and compatible to work with. Companies value soft skills because research suggests and experience shows that they can be just as important an indicator of job performance as hard skills. (Lorenz, 2009)

Can you generate a list of specific soft skills?

Michelle Roccia, a senior vice president of corporate organizational development, also makes judgments about potential employees using soft skills:

> When interviewing candidates to join our firm, two things can be deal breakers: attitude and core values. You can't teach attitude, but you can teach skill. A positive attitude, strong work ethic and strong values should trump more experience and skill. I also make sure the candidate demonstrates our company's core values. I ask them to tell me their "story" of their professional journey. Through their story, I get a better understanding of the decisions they made and the values they have (or don't have). (quoted in Zupek, 2010)

The requirements for making a good first impression vary from one corporation to the next as well as from one national culture to another. For instance, in U.S. culture, we exchange business cards after a meeting is completed. In some cultures, however, people exchange business cards as you meet someone for the first time. If you don't know the customs of the culture of an interviewer, you could eliminate yourself from consideration in the first few moments of an encounter. If you do any business travel or have the potential to meet people from another culture, you should research the other culture carefully to determine what you need to do to make a positive first impression.

The word *culture* also applies to the various departments and management levels within a company. Each department possesses a customary way of conducting business, using time, verbal jargon, and appearance. As you walk through different departments and floors of a building, you should observe a slightly different "look" in the people employed in each unit. Being aware of corporate culture and its variations assists you in making better decisions regarding which part of the company meets your future goals and needs.

ANSWERING QUESTIONS EFFECTIVELY

Now that you have made a good first impression, you need to follow through by sounding intelligent and professional when you speak. You must be aware of your nonverbals such as volume, rate, and inflection. Some people speak very loudly or very quickly when they are nervous, which can be annoying to others and could lower their perceptions of your credibility and competence. In addition to paying attention to how you speak, you should consider what you will say. Practice your answers to potential questions for coherency and uniqueness. The more you practice creating an engaging answer to various questions, the better prepared you will be to articulate excellent responses in an interview.

It is essential that your answers to various questions demonstrate that you have a basic understanding of the company and the position you are seeking. Research is imperative. Let's say you are interviewing for a job at a famous ice-cream company and you ask, "So what varieties of ice cream do you manufacture?" or "How many employees are in your company?" The immediate impression is that you aren't prepared. An interviewer would obviously think, "If you can't take the time to look up simple facts, why should I consider you for this job? You are wasting my time."

Behavioral interviewing is a common professional tool. In a behavioral interview, employers expect interviewees to provide detailed stories that demonstrate competence in a particular area (Half, 1993). Recruiters value behavioral interviews as an employment tool because applicants showcase their oral communication skills, interpersonal skills, critical-thinking skills, leadership skills, and teamwork skills (Moody, Stewart, and Bolt-Lee, 2002). To be successful at behavioral interviewing, candidates must be prepared to use personal stories to demonstrate their competence for the job in a meaningful and memorable way.

You must tell a compelling 1–2 minute personal story as you answer questions. We define *story* as an answer that has *characters*, a *plot*, a *climax*, and a *resolution*. If you answer the question, "What is your greatest strength?" with "I'm very calm under pressure; I can really get the job done; I don't sweat the small stuff," you haven't said anything. The interviewer will recognize these clichés but never remember your name. There is no way you can make a good impression with that simplistic answer.

Instead, let's consider a behavioral response to the same question. When the interviewer asks Veronica that question, she answers with a one-minute story. "Well, I'm very calm under pressure. For example, when I was working at the ice-cream shop, a customer received a cone that had a hole in it. It was a small hole in the bottom, but the ice cream began to drip through it, because it was a hot day. The woman was so irate that the ice cream had dripped on her suit, she came up to me and threw the ice cream in my face. I had to stand there in front of other customers and handle the situation without losing my cool. My first reaction was to get really angry and say something I would have regretted, but I bit my tongue, wiped off my face, and said very nicely, "Is something wrong?" And with that, all of the other customers turned their heads and stared at her. Once the focus was on her rather than on her actions, she stormed out of the ice-cream shop. While I was disappointed I couldn't make her happy, at least the other customers complimented me on the way I handled the situation."

Note that this is a 1–2 minute behavioral answer. It meets all of the criteria of storytelling in that it has characters, a plot, a climax, and a resolution. It paints a visual picture the interviewer is not likely to forget. Plus, it answers the question creatively. This type of answer makes Veronica memorable to the interviewer and much more likely to be remembered when the discussion regarding final candidates for the position takes place.

ETHICAL ENCOUNTERS

An interviewer looks at one of the employment sources on your résumé and asks you to describe a situation you thought represented your best accomplishment during employment. Unfortunately, the source they ask you about is a company where you actually accomplished nothing and even hated being there. Therefore, you decide to invent a situation to answer the question rather than admit the truth. What are some of the potential risks in telling a story like this?

Some of the basic questions you should be prepared to answer in a standard interview are:

1. Why should we hire you?
2. What is your greatest strength?
3. What is your greatest weakness?
4. What accomplishment has given you the greatest satisfaction?
5. What motivates you to put forth your greatest effort?
6. Why do you want to work for our company?

However, as more and more interviewers are looking for behavioral interview answers, you may find that you are asked questions that lead you directly to a story, such as:

7. Tell me how you handled your last conflict.
8. Tell me about a time when you had to work on a team.
9. Tell me about the last time you had to handle a really stressful situation.

You can find an extensive list of additional interview questions in the appendix.

As you create your answers to these questions while preparing for an interview, always keep your interviewer in mind—just as you think about your audience in public speaking. You shape your answers for the interviewer. If you answer, "Why do you want to work for our company?" with "Because I really need a job," or "Because I find this company to be prestigious," you are not thinking about your audience. Your answer is quite egocentric; a better answer reveals personal, skill-based information that makes you useful to the company. It is important to articulate how your greatest strength can benefit the corporation. A personal story about your dependability and how that quality will benefit the employer works to your advantage.

As you get ready to create your stories, it will be helpful for you to prepare a list of your skills and personality traits (refer to the statements you made about yourself in chapter 2). Skills are competencies you've learned, such as computer programs, problem solving, or speaking a foreign language. Personality traits are desirable qualities you possess, such as being dependable, energetic, and detail oriented. Once you have developed your list of skills and personality traits, you can then create the stories to highlight them. Good stories will make you stand out as conversational and professional.

Sometimes the interviewer is looking for the ability to think creatively. In this situation, an interviewer may ask a **brainteaser**—an open-ended hypothetical question that tests the problem-solving ability of a potential employee and necessitates a factual, logical, descriptive answer. Brainteasers are common in interviews for creative jobs. William Poundstone (2003) gives the following example of a brainteaser: "How much does the ice in a hockey rink weigh?" He notes: "Why use logic puzzles, riddles, and impossible questions? The goal...is to assess a general problem-solving ability rather than a specific competency" (p. 20). Non-computer-related industries such as those that deal with the public or the law also use brainteasers. The goal of this type of interview question is to test your experience with problem solving as well as your ability to remain calm under pressure. Many brainteasers do not have a correct answer. Your verbal ability to piece together logical thoughts in an impromptu manner is important. The brainteaser is somewhat different from the expectations for behavioral interviewing. The details and sequential logic in your answer to the brainteaser need to impress the interviewer.

Amy Lynn Keimach, an account manager, tells the following story about unexpected interview questions.

> During the interview process we tend to ask oddball questions and gauge [a candidate's] reaction and the actual answers they give. This will give us an idea as to how they will fit with our company and everyone else who works with us. For the upcoming semester we chose one intern over the others solely based on her answer to "If you were a candy bar, what kind would you be?" She sat for about three seconds but didn't think we were crazy for asking it. She smiled and said "I'd be a Caramello because they're awesome and hard to find, but when you find them you get a happy feeling inside." (quoted in Zupek, 2010)

The answer shows a lot of self-confidence. Keep in mind, though, not everyone would like that answer. Another person might answer, "I'd be a Hershey bar. I'm not trendy. I'm simple and straightforward, and have a history of consistent quality. What you see is what you get." Which answer do you like best?

Asking Effective Questions

Part of an effective interview is being prepared to ask good questions. You will meet many people on the day of your interview who will ask you if you have any questions, and if you sit there silently or say "no," you will not be perceived as an engaged and inquisitive candidate.

There are a number of questions that you can ask; feel free to ask the same questions more than once if you interview with different people. Here are some questions that will make you appear intelligent and engaged:

- What are you seeking in the ideal candidate for this position?
- How would you describe your management style?
- What do you like best about working for this organization?
- What would you like to see happen 6-to-12 months after you hire a new person for this position?
- What is your vision for the department over the next 2–3 years?
- Are there any weaknesses in the department you're working on improving?
- How is performance measured and reviewed?
- What's the single most important challenge facing your staff/ organization right now?

Obviously there are many more questions that you can create. You want to be fully prepared to ask questions based on your research about the company and its employees. Solid preparation will eliminate the dead space when someone asks you, "And what questions can we answer for you?"

Illegal Interview Questions

There are a number of **illegal interview questions**. It is illegal for interviewers to ask these questions, but sometimes they do anyway. You'll need to decide ahead of time what you will do if an employer asks you an illegal question. The following questions are from HR World (2010), and the article gives in-depth explanations about why each of these is illegal.

1. Are you a U.S. citizen?
2. What is your native tongue?
3. How long have you lived here?
4. What religion do you practice?
5. Which religious holidays do you observe?
6. Do you belong to a club or social organization?

7. How old are you?

8. How much longer do you plan to work before you retire?

9. What is your maiden name?

10. Do you have or plan to have children?

11. Can you get a babysitter on short notice for overtime or travel?

12. Do you have kids?

13. Who is your closest relative to notify in case of an emergency?

14. What do your parents do for a living?

15. If you get pregnant, will you continue to work, and will you come back after maternity leave?

16. We've always had a man/woman do this job. How do you think you will stack up?

17. How do you feel about supervising men/women?

18. What do you think of interoffice dating?

19. Do you smoke or drink?

20. Do you take drugs?

21. How tall are you?

22. How much do you weigh?

23. How many sick days did you take last year?

24. Do you have any disabilities?

25. Have you had any recent or past illnesses or operations?

26. How far is your commute?

27. Do you live nearby?

28. Have you ever been arrested?

29. Were you honorably discharged from the military?

30. Are you a member of the National Guard or Reserves?

If an interviewer asks an illegal question, you are in a difficult situation. You can point out that it is an illegal question, side step the question, or simply answer it. None of those three choices yields particularly good results. While you can prepare yourself for the possibility of an illegal question, the best procedure may depend on the specific situation—meaning you may need to decide what you want to do when the question arises.

COMMUNICATING AFTER THE INTERVIEW

It is essential that you use the utmost caution when writing to a prospective employer. Be absolutely sure to get the correct spelling of the interviewer's name and title while you are at the interview. You will need this information—and it must be accurate—to send a handwritten note after the interview. One misspelling in a thank-you note or e-mail will reveal additional information about your abilities. Handwritten notes are more personal and may be more appropriate for some employment opportunities. If you decide to write an e-mail thank-you (for example, after interviewing with a technology company), proofread carefully. Do not rely on spell-check programs alone—if you have mistakenly typed the wrong word but it is a word found in the dictionary, spell-check will not identify the error (for example, "principal" instead of "principle").

Keith Baumwald, an interactive marketing analyst, states, "One of the big things for me is [following] up. If I'm on the fence about a candidate but they take the time to e-mail me and thank me for having them come in, it shows me that they are motivated, tactful, and professional" (quoted in Zupek, 2010).

As a student, you may not think about the personal implications that are present when someone agrees to give you a reference or to help you make a professional connection. Rather than just providing a critical assessment of your skills, the person is putting his or her reputation on the line. Inappropriate or unprofessional behavior on your part reflects poorly on the person recommending you. Many professors and professionals are extremely cautious about giving recommendations because they have been burned by students and other colleagues. A recommendation is a transaction involving mutual respect. If Professor Yip gives Dominick a contact person, Dominick is obligated to contact that person and to let Professor Yip know he has followed through. Additionally, it is respectful to keep Professor Yip informed throughout the process, since she put her reputation on the line to help Dominick. A thank-you note to Professor Yip would also be in order. Networking is important; make sure you respond appropriately to someone's efforts on your behalf to expand potential networks rather than constricting them through poor behavior.

ETHICAL ENCOUNTERS

A professor gives you a contact for an interview and agrees to be your reference. You attend the interview and discover that the position isn't of interest to you so you give perfunctory answers so the interview ends quickly. You don't thank the interviewer for her time or tell your professor about the meeting. What you don't know is that the business contact is a former student of your professor. What scenarios can develop from this sequence of events?

FINAL THOUGHTS

Remember that job-related communication is a package deal. Strong written materials will help you secure a job interview. But once you walk into a corporate environment, the employment pendulum swings away from your writing to your appearance and verbal communication skills and style. You must concentrate on verbal and nonverbal messages throughout your exposure to a potential employer. Potential employers will remember everything you do and say. Practice and improve your written and oral skills while you are still in school. Remember to concentrate on your vocal technique at all times during phone interviews. Electronic interviews focus on only a portion of the communication package. Vocal technique and use of paralanguage become your selling points. It is important to develop your oral communication skills as soon as possible to make them effective. Sell your ability during an interview in a warm and friendly way. Personal stories are an engaging way to keep the interviewer interested in your message. Your professional future depends on consistent communication skills and style.

KEY TERMS

Artifact
Behavioral interviewing
Brainteaser
First impression
Illegal interview questions

Interviewing
Phone interview
Skype interview
Stress interview

EXERCISES

1. Schedule an appointment with a human resource person at a company to conduct an informative interview. What do they look for in selecting a person for a position? What legal issues do they face during the interview process? How many areas within the company hire entry-level personnel?

2. Pair students and have them interview each other in a timed format before the class. Classmates should critique the strengths and weaknesses of everyone at the end of the round.

3. Depending on the technical facilities available on campus, schedule a phone or a Skype interview with a classmate.

4. Each student should take a turn at the front of the class to respond to a typical interview question and to give a two-minute answer to a behavioral interview question.

Chapter

5

Basic Skills for the First Week

GOALS

After reading this chapter you should be able to:

✓ Explain the concept of impression management

✓ Assess your own use of impression management

✓ Define a brand

✓ Assess your own personal brand and rate its effectiveness

✓ Explain the concept of stereotyping

✓ Analyze problems with stereotyping in the workplace

✓ Explain the concept of self-disclosure

✓ Analyze the effectiveness of your own use of self-disclosure

✓ Compare and contrast hearing and listening

✓ Differentiate among the six listening styles

✓ Assess the implications of different listening styles in the workplace

✓ Explain the difference between fact and inference

✓ Examine your skill in attributing meaning

✓ Describe a good conversationalist

The anticipation of working at a new job site can be both exciting and somewhat nerve wracking. It is quite normal to question whether your experience is substantial enough to handle the job, whether your personality will blend with corporate goals, and whether your technical skills are strong enough to handle the workload. As unsettling as your intrapersonal thoughts may be, the reality of landing a job is that other people enjoyed meeting you and thought your résumé and skills fit the position they were trying to fill quite well. They selected you to assist them in advancing their business goals. Now, it is up to you to convince them that they made the right choice by hiring you.

Your first week of employment is a time where you will meet new colleagues, discover numerous workplace procedures, and figure out your actual workload as well as the communication structure of the company. There will be a ton of new information to absorb rapidly. Therefore, it is important to listen carefully to the instructions you receive and to observe keenly the activities unfolding around you so you blend in professionally. How you conduct yourself in the early days of employment can make or break the first impression others form regarding your ability, credibility, and potential for advancement within the organization.

ETHICAL ENCOUNTERS

A colleague states that it is fine to do personal business on company time. Should you use your computer for private, social communication?

IMPRESSION MANAGEMENT AND BRANDING

As you prepare for your first day of work, try to recall what colleagues were wearing when you went for your interview. You want to make sure that you dress appropriately for the workplace. You'll be meeting new people daily, and they will form first impressions about you based on how you look and how you behave. **Impression management** is "the process of managing setting, words, nonverbal communication, and dress in an effort to create a particular image of individuals and situations" (Wood, 2004, pp. 119–120). The term was introduced by Irving Goffman and suggests a personal commitment to excellence in verbal and nonverbal communication, whether the situation entails a formal presentation or a casual conversation with a colleague.

Impression management is a concept taught in communication theory classes, but businesses use the concept as well. The corporate world labels this concept as **"brand"** or **"branding."** Brands come in three categories: **corporate, project,** or **personal**. First, every business, school or university, political party, and religious establishment creates a brand for itself to communicate to the public and manage its image. Second, companies brand their products through their promotion, advertising, marketing, product's name, and physical appearance. Third, individuals themselves have brands. Celebrities, politicians, corporate executives, religious leaders, and everyday citizens brand themselves with their appearance, verbal ability, and ability to be noticed by others. It is useful to recognize the concept of branding so you can successfully brand yourself. You can enjoy certain positive social and professional rewards by making daily efforts to project a competent image of yourself. Everyone you meet and work with is doing exactly the same thing. As you decide what to wear to an event, monitor your language around certain audiences, or decide on the thank-you note design you will send, you are managing the impression you make.

We form first impressions in seconds. Your colleagues will make judgments about you, and you will make judgments about the people around you. As a new employee, it is extremely important to keep your fundamental nature in check and to keep an open mind about everyone you meet and everything you see. Time is your ally in making appropriate judgments about colleagues and corporate policies. Absorbing and analyzing stimuli prior to communication will enhance the accuracy of your assessments and make you more effective in the workplace. Projecting a consistent image and behaving professionally will help others perceive you as someone with whom they want to work.

We had a student who introduced us to the concept of a **personal representative**. Her mother warned her in her early teens that she would never really get to know the inner feelings or true nature of anyone she met in life. Her mother was a wise woman. All you will ever be entitled to know is what others allow you to know about them. Therefore, when you meet others, and as they meet you, each of you is encountering the other's personal representative. We all use impression

When starting a new job in an environment that has been working well and the employees all know each other, it is key for you not to "stir the pot" during your first week.

✓ Watch your mouth—you do not know the people there so don't curse up a storm.

✓ Use your "vault"—if someone tells you something (positive or negative) about someone else in the office or you hear gossip about others, keep it to yourself.

✓ Don't immediately reinvent their corporate wheel—let the employees there show you what they have been doing whether you agree with it or not and do it their way. When you have been there for a while, then you can provide other ideas or different ways of achieving a goal.

✓ Respect everyone—whether it's a vice president or the person who cleans the bathroom. You don't know interoffice relationships or friendships. Disrespecting the wrong person could put you in a negative light with someone you haven't even spoken to yet.

✓ Know and respect the rules—some places have unions that don't allow you to turn on a TV. Just because someone else does something doesn't mean the behavior is acceptable.

✓ Ask questions—if you need something or don't know how to do something, ask. Don't waste time; find out how to do your job as efficiently as possible.

Stephen Daily
Associate Producer
Fox Sports South

management as we send our personal representative forward on the first day of work.

Business is a team effort, and it takes time to understand colleagues and corporate policy. Your communication and behavior must reflect consistent professional standards of conduct. Work experience and your education give you the building blocks to shape the person you present to the world as worthy of employment. The business environment is not a social club. Your job is to earn a salary while making money for a company as well as improving its image.

So how do you do all this? As you walk into the building on your first day, there are a few perceptual choices to keep in check as you meet people and evaluate your corporate environment. Think of the job as a new beginning while leaving elements of the past behind you.

STEREOTYPING

Stereotyping is the act of labeling or treating people with similar characteristics as though they all exhibit the same values, judgments, and behavior. We also use labeling for the artifacts individuals wear and use in their personal space. We use perceptual judgments constantly to decide whom we think we will like as well as what we would like to see in an environment and do as an activity. We often base our perceptual decisions on experiences in the past rather than on the reality of the present. But it is important to put on the brakes to such automatic categorization in the workplace. A rush to judgment of another person or situation can prove fatal during a career. We experience sensory stimuli daily and categorize the stimuli by comparing them to what we already believe is true. Stereotyping develops from information we choose to hear and remember from our family, peers, religious establishments, teachers, community, and the entertainment media. Because stereotyping ignores the possibility of individual differences, it can be problematic, especially in the workplace. For example, thirty years ago society stereotyped men who wore earrings as homosexual. Then, a transition period occurred during which people interpreted earrings as a statement of sexual preference depending on whether the man wore the earring in the left or the right ear. Today men wear earrings without anyone automatically stereotyping them as gay.

As another example, years ago, when people saw a tattoo, they assumed the individual had a military background (usually the navy or marines) or had served time in prison. Tattoos are now more commonly regarded as skin art and part of mainstream society. Young people, parents, and some grandparents proudly display various creative designs on nearly every part of their bodies. However, you cannot assume that because tattoos are much more prevalent that everyone accepts them. People might not jump to conclusions about a military or criminal record, but they will base their reaction to you on their impressions about people who alter their bodily appearance. Some colleagues at work may be slightly unnerved by your tattoo simply because it is not part of their perception of what a person representing their company should look like. Some people will think your look is fine, while others may not like your look at all.

Stereotyping is something many of us do without thinking. Because we must organize stimuli during the perceptual process, stereotyping is a quick and easy way to group and analyze information. However, we have choices when it comes to assigning meaning to stimuli based on past stereotypes. While stereotypes allow us to organize information, they can also limit our ability to look at people and situations clearly. This lack of objectivity could lead to communication misunderstandings in a diverse workforce. Once you recognize your stereotypical beliefs while maintaining perceptual flexibility, you become better equipped to communicate effectively with business colleagues and global clients.

Think carefully about yourself for a minute and think about what attributes you are most likely to notice about others. How do you think people might stereotype you on the first day of the job? Is your voice commanding or breathy—what are the stereotypes? Do you project an air of confidence or mousiness as you meet someone or enter a space? Stereotypical thinking exists, and you want to do everything possible to present the best possible image to new colleagues to manage the impression they will form of you.

In some businesses, your supervisor will escort you around the building and introduce you to a number of employees. In other work-places, your coworker may show you to your office and expect you to get to work with little fanfare. Thus, you need to figure out tasks on your own and complete the assignments handed to you. It's also possi-ble that a portion of your first day will involve a visit to human resources to go over paperwork and corporate procedures as well as receive your security badge. Whether someone else introduces you or you end up introducing yourself, you know that meeting coworkers is the first item on the agenda the very first day. You don't want anyone to stereotype you negatively because of your appearance or behavior. As you anticipate the routine on your first day, you also need to anticipate what you are going to say as conversations begin.

SELF-DISCLOSURE

You enter the office space that you will share with a coworker. How do you get to know one another? Most people begin with a brief introduction: exchange names, nice to meet you, and so on. Additional information about an office mate is not necessary since you are there to do a job. Social events like lunch and continuous days of working together will allow for a greater exchange of background information between colleagues. **Self-disclosure** is the act of voluntarily giving personal information to another person. You need to disclose information about yourself in order to give others a feeling for who you are. Revealing information about your background and philosophy of life can strengthen interpersonal relationships. However, effective disclosure of personal information is done slowly and over a long period of time.

What are some of the common things we disclose when we first meet a colleague? Our name, where we graduated from school, and work experience we've had prior to the current job are typical topics for self-disclosure. Some initial self-disclosures are appropriate or inappropriate depending on the region of the country in which one lives. For example, when I (KSY) moved to Arkansas, I was in the car with a colleague and her 7-year-old daughter. The daughter looked at me and asked, "What church do you go to?" I waited for the mother to correct her daughter for asking an inappropriate question. From my perspective, the question was too intimate for initial self-disclosure. Silence reigned, however. The mother was actually waiting for me to answer the question since in that region of the country, at that time, "What church do you go to?" was usually the second question asked of strangers, immediately after asking "What is your name?" The silence was extremely awkward because both of us were waiting for the other person to speak. A moment like this is a simple reminder of how self-disclosure can vary from one region of the country to another and why it is important to maintain an open mind in all communication.

We have choices about the depth of information and the amount of intimate information we disclose to strangers. There is no specific formula for what is appropriate and what is inappropriate to say during a conversation. People can share personal information regarding their past if they choose to do so, but the specific choices and their details vary from person to person. For example, technology offers a platform where many individuals openly share personal information rarely discussed in a business environment. Technology eliminates the need to wade through years of social discourse to discover a new colleague's background. Employers and others can check social networking sites instantly to discover what someone is doing or thinking about, their religious and political backgrounds, and the things they like to do. Therefore, it is important to review the material on your social networking sites to make sure it matches the impression you are trying to create professionally through impression management. The willingness of people to share personal information with strangers is changing rapidly with new media and a younger generation's shift in communication style.

One way to gauge the appropriateness of self-disclosure is by interpreting the nonverbal behavior of your conversation partner. People may demonstrate discomfort with your self-disclosure through their vocalizations, their silence, lowering eye contact with you, or a sudden shift of subject matter. When this nonverbal/verbal change occurs during a conversation, you need to be perceptive enough to stop your content disclosure immediately. If you are in a position where someone is disclosing information and expecting you to disclose similar details, you may find it necessary to respond in a very calm manner with something like, "I'm not prepared to talk about that right now. Can we please change the subject?" This is a reasonable way to let the other person know he or she has overstepped the bounds of appropriate discussion without closing off further communication. People have different tolerances for what constitute appropriate topics for daily conversation. If you have not yet reached the same comfort level for disclosure of a content area, communicate how you feel while leaving the door open for the relationship to continue.

Please remember that some disclosures must happen for collegial relationships to grow. Some people find it difficult to disclose anything personal or philosophical in a social/business setting, and yet, reveal a great deal about themselves on social media sites. It is extremely difficult to build a working relationship with colleagues who never self-disclose how or why they solve problems or reach conclusions the way they do. Business conversations should always remain professional. It is important to remember that gender research supports the general conclusion that men tend to self-disclose much less than women do (Ivy and Backlund, 2004, p. 212). Men and women need to solve problems and develop business strategies with the same degree of mental energy, but their levels of disclosure about how they reach conclusions may vary. How you decide to work verbally/nonverbally with a colleague of the opposite gender is a decision only you can make. But, always be prepared for the consequences of your choices.

ETHICAL ENCOUNTERS

A colleague shares personal information with you during lunch. The information demonstrates behavior that is against corporate policy. Do you share the information with your boss to gain favor?

The more intimate the information you choose to share, the greater the trust you must have in the other person. While intimate self-disclosure can make personal working relationships closer, it also makes you vulnerable should the other person deliberately choose to violate your confidence. You should weigh the risks before sharing information with another person. Unfortunately, we learn the lesson of what is an acceptable risk with life experience. There are moments when you may get burned by others, but it's a risk you must take when you feel someone is worth knowing at work or socially. Trust in others involves risk. If someone violates your trust, you will at least know that you were willing to participate in open, honest communication with someone else. Although withholding certain information may be prudent in numerous circumstances, silence will not lead to close relationships.

OBSERVATION

In a business setting, you are responsible for figuring out what you are supposed to do, therefore listening carefully to what is going on around you and observing how the office works are critical skills in becoming a professional person. For example, your exposure to memos, e-mails, and in-house documents will be immediate. You should read every piece of printed information that crosses your desk or computer screen carefully. Careful examination will reveal the format and writing style of both the company and the sender. It is easy to establish a bond with someone if you respond to messages in the same format and writing style. Although your writing style sets you apart from colleagues, it doesn't hurt to be cognizant of how other individuals write. A simple stylistic alteration can set you apart from other people in the company immediately. How do others use clauses, adverbs, adjectives, verb tenses, and so on? People will be more comfortable reading your responses to their messages when your writing ability is similar to theirs. We cover other writing concepts in the next chapter to help you be successful.

ETHICAL ENCOUNTERS

Do you mention or discuss internal policies shared in a closed meeting with members of your family? Your significant other?

After your first day at work, you should read the corporate information given to you by human resources as well as all corporate policy procedures. Your understanding of these manuals will save you the embarrassment of making mistakes when communicating at work. Reasonable questions to clarify a statement or procedure are fine, but they have hired you as an experienced professional, and your colleagues and supervisors are not there to teach you business etiquette, style, and behavior. They expect you to work and think at their level from your first day forward.

LISTENING

Make sure to listen carefully when people introduce themselves to you or give you instructions. You don't want to ask them to repeat themselves nor do you want to struggle to remember names later. Others will assume that you have retention skills. Therefore, if you have any question(s) about what you've heard, ask for clarification immediately. Confirmation of a name or point is better than a mistake later.

Most people are born with the ability to hear, but listening is an acquired skill. **Hearing** is a passive action. It is simply the process of sound hitting your eardrums. Think back to chapter 2 on perception. We talked about the concept of selective attention in response to the multitude of sounds that constantly bombard us. We hear everything, but we only pay attention to specific sounds based on personal need and preference. Initially, you need to treat every sound as important and strive to decode the messages accurately.

Chances are you really had a difficult time remembering the names of everyone you met on the initial office tour. This is because you were not actively listening to the names as people introduced themselves. **Listening** is an active process where you selectively attend to and assign meaning to sounds. If we analyzed every sound within earshot, we'd be overwhelmed. However, business situations require you to listen with a focus that may not be as necessary in many other aspects of your personal life. Once we focus on which sounds are critically important in our worklife, we can process the information and respond appropriately. The names of people you work with are important, and you should make a concerted effort to retain the information without having to ask again. One method to solidify the information is to repeat the name immediately: "It's really nice to meet you, Xiamara."

Being an effective listener is a skill that takes practice. Some of us develop this skill to a much finer degree than others do. Because every interpersonal business relationship is unique and because each communication situation has different listening requirements, we need to learn multiple listening styles in order to be a strong communicator. A review of listening and feedback styles should assist you in interpreting what you hear as well as understanding what responses are appropriate in daily communication.

Listening/Feedback Styles

Many communicators learn only one listening/ feedback style and use it consistently, but this rigidity doesn't allow for the uniqueness of situations. As you progress through many corporate situations, flexibility and the ability to adapt to new information immediately helps you to become an effective listener and stronger professional. There are six different listening/feedback styles. Some of them are more useful than others, but each one serves a purpose. The six styles are judgmental, questioning, directive, empathetic, interpreting, and active. We will illustrate each of the stylistic choices with the following scenario. Frank approaches his colleagues and says: "I can't believe my performance review states that I need to improve my problem-solving skills, and I am not as team-oriented as I should be."

Judgmental listening/feedback means a listener makes a judgment about both the content and the speaker. Judith, who is a judgmental listener, tells Frank: "Well, I told you that you needed to present better analysis of the research in our meetings." This response makes Judith sound superior because she "knew it all along." It also implies that Frank was negligent in not knowing what to do to make a good impression.

Questioning is another listening/feedback style. The listener asks probing questions of the speaker that are not necessarily supportive questions. They sometimes have a hint of accusation in their tone. Frank's office mate is a questioning listener and asks, "Why didn't you show up on time at our last meeting and present some research to back up your argument?" While he is inviting more conversation, he is also placing a confrontational edge on the communication. He is implying that Frank did something wrong. This leads Frank to reply defensively.

Both questioning and judgmental listening/feedback styles serve to put down the other person without lending any support. They are not typically useful in the workplace.

Directive listening/feedback means a listener tells the speaker what to do. Giovanni tells Frank: "Well, the first thing you need to do is present an original solution to a discussion. Then you need to . . ." As a directive listener, Giovanni tries to solve the problem by giving advice.

Empathetic listening/feedback means a listener gives the speaker an emotional form of support. Sarah says, "Oh, Frank, I'm so sorry. You must feel awful. Is there anything I can do?" Sarah, an empathetic listener, tries to comfort Frank.

Directive and empathetic listening can be useful depending on the needs of the speaker. If you want to be emotionally comforted, empathetic feedback is great, while directive feedback feels like the person isn't listening. If you want to solve the problem, directive feedback is terrific, while empathetic feedback sounds condescending.

Did you think Giovanni's and Sarah's responses were stereotypical? We intentionally chose to use a male for directive listening and a female for empathetic listening because, in general, women are more likely to be empathetic listeners while men are more likely to be directive listeners (Wood, 2011, pp. 128–131).

The **interpreting** style of listening/feedback means a listener tries to offer another explanation of what happened. This style can be very useful in helping the speaker to think of other possible explanations for an event or a better analysis of the problem. Svetlana tells Frank, "Maybe your supervisor made a mistake. Did you think about going in to ask for specific examples of how you can meet their image of a better problem solver?" As an interpretive listener, Svetlana helps Frank explore other possibilities for his dilemma.

Active listening/feedback means a listener offers supportive questions and is clearly willing to listen. The listener tries to encourage more communication, using paraphrasing to ensure understanding. There are two useful types of paraphrasing. You may use a content-level paraphrase or a relationship-level paraphrase. A **content paraphrase** summarizes the message the other person states. The **relationship paraphrase** checks on the emotional state of the speaker.

Content paraphrase: "Oh wow, I'm sorry, so are you saying you might lose your job if you don't improve immediately?"

Relationship (emotional) paraphrase: "Oh my, you sound really upset. Would you like to talk about what happened?"

The active listener may use either or both of these styles if they are appropriate. In many situations, you may not need either. Active listening helps the speaker emotionally process his/her reaction to a situation or talk through ways to solve a problem. It doesn't superimpose a plan. The active listener acts as a sounding board and allows the speaker to discover the best solution for the dilemma.

In addition to becoming more effective as an employee by consistently using the appropriate listening/feedback style, listening can also challenge you ethically. Let's say you are returning from lunch and while walking back to your office you pass a supervisor's door. The supervisor is talking on the phone and saying that a vice president of the company just ordered that the VP's daughter be hired to fill a job opening in your department. You were never supposed to hear this conversation. Sadly, someone you know applied for the position and even interviewed well for the job. The person you know has been out of work and is well qualified to work in your department, but she will be bypassed because of the inside hire. This situation is now an ethical challenge for you because you can't admit you overheard a private conversation, and you can't tell the person you know she is not getting the job due to a business confidentiality policy. Enforced silence isn't easy, and it can become a challenge, but it is necessary if you want to brand yourself as a professional.

This is an age when everyone is talking and no one is listening. If you put a priority on being a good listener, you may feel overburdened at times, but you will be unique in the crowd of people who want to be heard.

Implications of Styles

Communication misunderstandings occur when people don't receive the feedback style they are expecting. Think about how defensive you might get if you weren't expecting a questioning or judgmental response from a colleague. If you are looking for help, sympathy, or an active listener to help you out, a questioning or judgmental listener will make you feel worse or angry. At this point, communication stops or an argument may begin. Careful analysis of your colleagues will help you decide whom to ask when you have a question or concern. Approaching those who have a feedback response style that is comfortable for you will often be the best choice. In other situations, however, the person whose style differs from yours may be the most informed about a specific topic. If that is the case, be prepared *not* to react to the style but to listen to the content of the response.

The point above highlights the necessity to analyze yourself as well as your colleagues. If you really want a listener to give you a pity party, you will choose someone with an empathetic style. If that person changes course and begins directing you instead, you may feel the person is not really listening to what you are saying. In this situation, you already feel emotionally drained, and if the listener begins to give you directives, you may resent someone telling you what to do. All you really wanted from a listener was momentary sympathy. You expected one response but received another. Your analysis about styles may have been accurate, but each communication situation differs. The customarily empathic person may feel strongly about a particular topic and becomes directive. Being aware of such a possibility will help you be flexible if the feedback isn't what you expected.

Improving Listening Skills

There are some easy ways to improve your listening skills. When you are in a business meeting, maintain good posture, make eye contact with the speaker, and take lots of notes. Note taking keeps you focused on the message as you write. Make sure that you are knowledgeable about the material to be covered in a meeting and be prepared to discuss it (review and analyze everything on the agenda). Knowing the information makes listening easier. Of course, it is easier to concentrate during a meeting if the speaker is an excellent communicator and highlights the most important points—but not all business people are good presenters. A poor presentation does not mean you can nod off or demonstrate a lack of interest in the subject. Active listening will help you overcome shortcomings in the presentation.

The diverse workforce provides interesting challenges. When foreign-born colleagues speak English, they may have a challenging inflection pattern. Be aware of cultural uses of language, sound substitutions, and possible grammar variations as you listen to spoken language. You can perform tasks incorrectly if you fail to listen actively to a supervisor, client, or colleague who comes from a different cultural background. These situations are quite challenging for many people, but you can overcome them easily with active listening.

FACT VERSUS INFERENCE

As you are listening to coworkers and bosses and trying to assign meaning to perceived events, it is imperative to realize the difference between factual statements and inferential statements. Once again, listening is the key to responding properly. **Facts** are observable phenomena. Observation reveals the existence of say, the office furniture around you: a desk, a chair, and a lamp. **Inferences** are conclusions we draw about the facts we observe. For instance, if the furniture in your workspace is brand new, you might infer that you are an important part of the organization and a valued addition to the company. On the other hand, if your furniture is old and tired in appearance, you might infer that you are an afterthought or the company is in financial trouble. We draw conclusions about our surroundings automatically. When you begin to interact with others and get a truer sense of your value to the company, you will realize your inferences are right or wrong. If we act as though a perception is fact when it is actually inference, we can create numerous communication problems for ourselves.

Confusing fact with inference directly relates to the interpretation step of the perceptual process. Be aware that emotional reactions to past and present experiences affect our inferences. We may infer meaning based on how we feel rather than on what we actually see. The conclusion based on feeling may often be incorrect. Let's say you are supposed to meet your office mate at a local restaurant around 5:00 P.M. You show up a little early and are surprised to find your office mate hugging an attractive person, and you notice empty cocktail glasses on the table. You feel like you are intruding and are very uncomfortable. Your office mate sees you hesitate and waves for you to join them. The expression on your face makes it clear that they need to explain the situation. The attractive person turns out to be a cousin who happened to be having dinner at the same restaurant, and they were sharing a cocktail before you arrived. Your emotional reaction of being an unwelcome third party affected your inferences about your office mate's personal life.

ETHICAL ENCOUNTERS

What if the colleague is married and this had, in fact, been a romantic encounter with someone else? What do you do?

ATTRIBUTING MEANING

When we witness the behaviors of others, we try to make sense of those behaviors and assign meaning to them. **Attribution** happens when we create meaning for behaviors. It is very likely that from observation alone, we can never know for sure what behaviors mean, but we often feel confident about our interpretations. The process of attributing meaning can easily result in miscommunication.

For example, Laquaan sees Tina talking on her office phone as he walks past the door. Tina glances at him and quickly turns away without responding and lowers her voice. He feels ignored and interprets her action as a snub. She normally waves to everyone as they pass her door and often says, "Hello." Laquaan immediately thinks Tina is hiding something from him because her behavior is unusual. An emotional reaction to the encounter clouds his judgment. "Fine," he thinks and proceeds down the hallway. He assumes Tina intentionally ignored him, but is his assumption correct?

Laquaan has choices as he analyzes the situation. He can act as though his assumption is fact. Or, he can question his assumption immediately. He may also brainstorm for other reasons that would explain Tina's action. Or, he can be more direct and active by checking his perceptions (see the section on perception checking in chapter 2). Laquaan would benefit from attributing reasons other than ignoring him to Tina's actions or doing a perception check immediately. The decisions you make about business colleagues and their behavior should always be factual. Assumptions can make you appear odd, ridiculous, or arrogant. It is best to analyze communication and/or behavior prior to responding to it. Everyone who experiences your poor communication will remember your error in judgment.

THE ART OF CONVERSATION

Conversation is an interpersonal exchange demonstrating your ability to be engaging with others while asking appropriate questions of them as well as responding to their inquiries of you. Good conversation involves intense listening to messages and their intent in spontaneous dialogue. The spontaneous nature of conversation on a variety of topics appears to be a relic of past generations with today's overabundance of one-liners, e-mails, tweets, and focus on self rather than another person. Therefore, possessing the skills necessary for conducting a stimulating, social conversation is an excellent way to stand out in the business world.

Have you ever been in the presence of someone who rambles on constantly about what he is doing? What he is thinking? Where he is going on vacation? How much he is spending on meals? Why his job is horrible and he deserves better? During the time you are with this person, does he ever ask you how you are doing or feeling about anything? If so, this experience cannot be called a conversation. It is simply a monologue. This communicator does not want your response to any of the issues raised during the monologue. We call this person a spewer. He simply spews information.

A conversation allows both participants to share facts, opinions, or feelings on a wide range of topics. A conversation usually begins with a thoughtful question from one person followed by a reasoned response from another person. Your ability to listen carefully while someone is responding to a question is crucial in making a conversation successful. Throughout the other person's response, you should locate an idea (fact, philosophy, word choice, etc.) that allows you to logically do a follow-up question/statement/comment on the same topic. This process allows both participants to fully explore an idea. The topic of a conversation usually changes during the time spent sharing ideas/thoughts while at the same time demonstrating a respect for the other person's point of view.

Conversational style is definitely enhanced when both participants use storytelling to color real-life experiences and make their response to questions interesting to hear. The ability to listen to what another person is saying and then find an appropriate verbal/nonverbal response allows conversation to seem effortless for both participants. This effortless, enjoyable quality of time spent talking to others is becoming an art form worthy of mastering to stand out in the workplace.

Daily conversations usually focus on mundane topics such as sports, weather, and traffic. But today, coworkers often talk in depth about topics like reading, time management, new technology, economic growth, diversity, global acquisitions, current news items, and competitive start-up companies. Today's workforce is expected to know a little bit about a wide range of issues/ideas. Most workplace discussions involve work-related themes. However, you may find yourself in a position to enter into social discussions with colleagues as well. These social discussions may involve time management issues related to family and work, hobbies and outside activities, current books you've read, or personal interests.

Think back to the previous discussion about listening. If you can incorporate active listening skills into a conversation, you will excel in making a good impression on someone. Many people want to talk about themselves. Personal monologues are not conversations. If, however, you have the opportunity to talk to your boss or other important people in the company, there are a couple of strategies that will help to make you memorable. These strategies include your ability to listen attentively, ask thoughtful questions that engage others, and allow others to talk. When other individuals walk away from a conversation with a positive feeling about the experience, you make a professional impression. You must also be able to project sincerity throughout a conversation with your use of language and tone of voice. Simply nodding your head while zoning out will not help your cause.

While it may sound silly, if you know you are going to have an opportunity for social conversation at a business gathering or happy hour, you should plan a couple of good questions to engage people in conversation. If you've been paying attention in the workplace, you should have picked up a few clues about what is important to other people or what their interests are. Even a simple, open-ended question such as, "So, how do you spend your free time?" can open up a conversational avenue that allows the person to talk for quite a while about something that is important to them.

Be aware that most people in today's society have so much going on that quite often they don't care about other people's stories. Therefore, it is helpful to recognize the difference between someone seeking a brief response to a statement and someone attempting to engage you in a conversation. One of the best ways to ingratiate yourself with someone else is to demonstrate that you care, to listen actively, and to engage him or her in further conversation. So few people do it, that the person you are conversing with will recognize the interpersonal experience as a unique situation.

Interpersonal conversations take time, which is one reason why people are uncomfortable having a productive conversation with someone else. People will sometimes try to start a conversation with you when you are not interested or lack the time to respond. When you have a timetable to follow, make an opening statement such as, "I have a meeting in five minutes, but I can talk to you until then." This tells someone upfront that your time is limited, but you are willing to chat. In other words, think before you speak and establish ground rules for time when they are necessary to maintain your personal schedule. It is important to be honest with your commitment of time as well as your listening and response skills for an interpersonal discussion to be called a conversation. Satisfying conversations should end with both participants appreciating the experience—feeling as though they were listened to and given appropriate responses.

TECHNOLOGY IN THE FIRST WEEK

You may be tempted to leave your personal phone on as you go to work the first day rather than silence it. However, you may not make a good impression on an employer if you take personal calls while at work, and some companies have policies against using a personal phone altogether. You'll have to learn company policies immediately. When can you use your cell phone/BlackBerry/iPhone? It is always safe to turn your personal device off and leave it alone unless you are on a break or lunch hour. While at the office, it may be best to avoid taking a personal call that is inappropriate and might be overheard. We are amazed at people who conduct personal business on their cell phones and give personal identification information (like a bank account number) or financial information over the phone when colleagues are within earshot.

> "The day will come when [people] will have to fight noise as inexorably as cholera and the plague."
> — Nobel Prize-winning bacteriologist Robert Koch, 1905
>   (quoted in Baird, 2010)

Joanna Krotz (n.d.) of Microsoft Corporation advises never taking a personal mobile call during a business meeting—including interviews and meetings with coworkers. She also suggests:

Maintain at least a 10-foot zone from anyone while talking. . . .
Never talk in elevators, libraries, museums, restaurants, cemeteries, theaters, dentist or doctor waiting rooms, places of worship, audito-

riums or other enclosed public spaces, such as hospital emergency rooms or buses. And don't have any emotional conversations in public—ever.

Numerous corporate structures contain hidden microphones as well as cameras in elevators, hallways, lobbies, offices, and bathrooms. They use this hidden technology to protect the company and its employees during an emergency situation. A business is a public space, and the employer is trying to keep you safe rather than spy on you, but security will hear your conversations. Use caution if you choose to conduct personal conversations while at your work site. Show consideration for the people around you, and if your conversations will be overheard, make sure the language is acceptable.

One of the pleasures of your first day on the job is using the automated phone system in your office to record a message that identifies the number as your own. The material given to you when you were hired describes the corporate protocol. The protocol tells you how to update or redirect your phone messages as well as when to do so. You will probably have an access code that enables you to reach your voice mail from various locations. This code allows you to retrieve messages while you are away from your desk so you can quickly respond to clients, colleagues, or management. Or you may have messages instantly forwarded to your personal phone. Voice mail messages in a business setting are as important as your computer or portable device. You'll need to check it on a regular basis and reprogram with specific scheduling information such as "I am out of the office this afternoon but I can be reached at…" The need to be able to respond immediately to messages increases as responsibility within an organization increases.

FINAL THOUGHTS

A job is a privilege rather than a rite of passage—whether it is the culmination of a high school/college education, a second career choice, or a new position. The financial recession that started in 2008 has increased the competitiveness of the global job market. Employers are examining the quality of candidates seeking employment more extensively than ever before—paying special attention to technology and communication skills as corporations go "virtual." The era of a five-day, forty-hour work week in an English speaking corporation is disappearing rapidly.

Technology opens the doors to individuals in any country who possess solid writing, verbal skills, analytical ability, and enthusiasm for employment. You need to absorb new ideas, skills, and ways of thinking faster than ever before to obtain a job or to avoid losing one. A personal commitment to lifelong learning can propel you ahead of colleagues who are slower to learn new skills or ways of thinking. Your ability to earn a comfortable salary, whatever that number is for you, will depend on your ability to adjust your skills and thinking to meet the demands of corporations, technology, and global markets. Mastering vital skills will improve both your competence and your confidence. Learn to take yourself seriously as a professional person and continue to expand your talent.

Kate Lorenz (2007) believes in the concept that attitude is a critical factor to being a successful worker. She recommends developing and maintaining the following beliefs, adapted from her article on the power of positive attitude:

1. **I am in charge of my destiny.**

   If you spend your entire career waiting for something exciting to come to you, you will be waiting a long time. Successful professionals go out and make good things happen. So commit yourself to thinking about your career in an entirely different way. You will make it to the top, and you are in charge of making it happen.

2. **No task is too small to do well.**

   You never know when you are going to be noticed. One public relations executive in Chicago said that her first task in the PR department of a ballet company was reorganizing the supply closet. She tackled the project with gusto and was immediately noticed for her hard work and attention to detail. No task is menial; take pride in your work—all of it.

3. **It's not just what I know, but who I know.**

   Successful workers understand the importance of networking, both in and out of the office. Proactively establish professional contacts: invite a colleague to lunch; go to the after-work happy hour; join your professional association. Do your part to establish a networking path for your future.

4. **Failure will help pave the way to my success.**

   While it seems like some people never experience setbacks, the truth is everyone fails from time to time. The difference between successful and unsuccessful people is how they deal with failure. Those who find success are the ones who learn from mistakes and move on.

5. **My opportunity monitor is never turned off.**
   There will be days when you are content with the status quo—but remember that successful workers are always on the lookout for opportunities to improve. Keep your eyes, ears, and your mind open to new opportunities. You never know when you will discover the one that will change the course of your career!

Your first job is the beginning of your financial future, so take it seriously. Consistent communication behavior will allow you to reach your goals in life. Mistakes happen when you don't think about what you are saying or doing. Acknowledge your mistakes; learn from them; and move forward. A new job is a wonderful opportunity to showcase your talent in a corporate setting. Therefore, choose to be successful and make the person who gave you that initial career opportunity proud they did so.

KEY TERMS

Active listening style
Attribution
Brand
Communication misunderstanding
Content paraphrase
Conversation
Directive listening style
Empathetic listening style
Fact
Hearing

Impression management
Inference
Interpreting listening style
Judgmental listening style
Listening
Personal representative
Questioning listening style
Relationship paraphrase
Self-disclosure
Stereotyping

EXERCISES

1. Analyze your personal "brand."
2. Analyze the image and language of a political spot and describe the facts versus inferences used in the spot.

3. Discuss your listening style. How can you improve?

4. Describe the extent of self-disclosure you find comfortable with strangers. Is this a wise decision?

5. Describe a time when someone disclosed information inappropriately in the workplace.

6. Discuss the most recent use of stereotyping in language and where you heard/saw it. Do you use stereotyping in your own communication?

6

Writing Skills and Technology for the First Week and Beyond

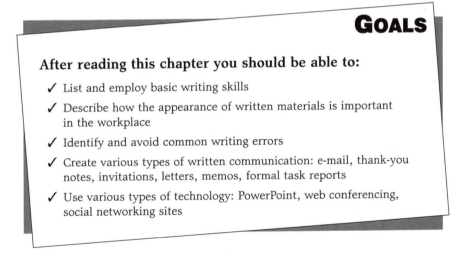

GOALS

After reading this chapter you should be able to:

- ✓ List and employ basic writing skills
- ✓ Describe how the appearance of written materials is important in the workplace
- ✓ Identify and avoid common writing errors
- ✓ Create various types of written communication: e-mail, thank-you notes, invitations, letters, memos, formal task reports
- ✓ Use various types of technology: PowerPoint, web conferencing, social networking sites

So now you are employed. Writing becomes a significant portion of your professional life. If you are lucky enough to have an executive assistant or office professional to edit your work, consider yourself a very fortunate person. But typically, anyone in an entry-level position is completely responsible for all of his or her written communication. Your personal credibility (chapter 2) is revealed each time you correspond with anyone as an employed person. Mistakes in written correspondence can affect your future within a company.

In college, your e-mails and texts weren't always judged for writing strength, but this situation changes in the workplace. A majority of business professionals will notice when you make simple spelling and/ or grammatical errors even while e-mailing or texting. Some people overlook these errors assuming that you are busy and in a hurry. But others will immediately come to the conclusion that you either don't know how to write or lack attention to detail. This conclusion will affect their perception of you as a business professional.

The degree to which you edit your written work is definitely your choice, but we recommend that you exercise care and diligence, especially if you are trying to establish yourself as a competent colleague. Quality writing can set you apart from numerous colleagues. It makes the most sense to be overly cautious when writing, editing, and sending anything in the workplace, since written documents are kept for legal reasons, copied, placed in files, forwarded to others, and so on. In addition, the appearance of written material is sometimes as important as its style.

BASIC WRITING SKILLS

Mastering these basic skills is a simple way to set yourself apart from your peers.

Terms

Draft.   You should head all working documents clearly with the word "Draft." This alerts colleagues to the fact your communication is a work in progress and that feedback is expected. Once they return their comments, rewrite the document, remove the word "draft," and forward the document.

Edit.   Everything you send to colleagues and clients alike should be free of typos and grammatical errors; it should be punctuated correctly. This statement also applies to team projects that contain your name. Therefore, read every report for accuracy prior to its release. Your entire team looks bad when written errors appear in the final report.

Research. Factual information contained in a document must be accurate. Computers make double checking facts and various sources much easier, so take the time to complete this task for all supporting material in the final document. Corporate files are usually available to you on a secure corporate intranet site. It is also possible that some business information may need to be researched in storage areas where paper files are located.

Read. Every document that crosses your desk and computer screen needs to be read and remembered. In most cases, you should save or copy important material for future reference. Your ability to keep up with the volume of information you receive is a tremendous challenge, but you must do it. Good record keeping will help you remember or locate trends, legal issues, policy changes and the dates they occurred. It can also be useful to remember the writing styles of important people around you so you can communicate with them electronically in their own style. When you receive the minutes of a business meeting, it is helpful to review them for accuracy. If you notice an error in the minutes, contact the session's recording secretary to have them corrected. Minutes of business meetings are legal documents and need to be accurate. As a participant in a meeting, you are just as responsible for accuracy in the minutes as the recording secretary, so be diligent as you review the material.

Nonverbal Appearance

As you create business materials, try to envision the nonverbal message they will send to colleagues and clients. The layout and design, quality of paper, binding, and visual quality of each item will communicate your attention to detail. This statement also applies to PowerPoint and other computer-generated graphics. A superior presentation encourages people to read carefully and think favorably of the material in addition to analyzing its content more carefully. When business materials appear to be sloppy, the content itself becomes questionable, and the desire to read it wanes significantly. Here are some simple tips to send the nonverbal message, "I am a competent professional":

- Use 20–25% cotton bond paper for important documents

- Make sure to print material so that the watermark is facing toward you and is upright

- Be sure that all holes are punched exactly alike so that pages line up if the document is put in a binder

- If you are stapling, be sure to tap papers well, so they are all exactly in line with one another
- Make sure the fonts are consistent and legible
- All tabs for dividers should be computer-generated
- No typos or grammatical errors
- In general, single-space paragraphs with double-spacing in between them
- If you are binding a document, use a 1.5 inch margin on the left side
- Cover designs should be simple and professional
- Clip art is generally not for use in professional design

While some of these suggestions may seem picky, they will contribute to your overall professional image.

Common Writing Errors

As your written communication with colleagues and clients begins, you want to be concise and clear—and flawless—with the messages you send. Employers expect educated employees to have solid writing skills. There are companies who give spelling tests to anyone applying for work in specific career areas, as well as for professional internal advancement. The idea of a corporate spelling test may seem startling, but these tests allow companies to make sure they are hiring the right person for the job. You can avoid common writing errors with proper attention to detail:

- Cite the source for absolutely everything you use and make certain the citation is accurate.
- Number all pages.
- Use headings and subheadings in your writing.
- Do not strand a heading at the bottom of a page—bump it to the next page.
- Use a preview and review if appropriate in the document.
- Professional reports normally look better with tab dividers, which should be printed (use your computer to format such projects).
- Watch for stylistic shifts when assembling group writing (i.e. team projects) and reformat for a uniform presentation.

- Be careful with spell-check. As mentioned previously, spell-check will catch typos, but it will not save you from using "there" instead of "their." In addition, look carefully at the options for changing a typo. The correct spelling for the word you intended may not be the first choice. Do not automatically choose "change."

- Eliminate the word "very" from your writing. Never use very, very.

- "Nowadays" should never appear in your business writing.

- "A lot" is two words (not alot).

- Join two complete sentences with a conjunction, preceded by a comma. "The dog ran, and the cat sat. The rat jumped, but he did not bite."

- Many compound adjectives are hyphenated before but not after a noun: "My hard-hearted boss would not give me a raise."

- When in doubt, consult a good dictionary.

- Do not use contractions in formal writing. "Don't" should be "do not."

- Create dashes by typing *two* hyphens with no space before or after the hyphens—see what I mean? (Software programs such as Microsoft Word can automatically convert two hyphens into the em dash [—], or find the special characters in your software program.)

- Refrain from using "all caps" in e-mails. All caps mean you are shouting.

- Use active rather than passive voice. "Raoul studied the reports carefully" vs. "The reports were studied by Raoul."

- Make sure that you read all of your written material out loud. This will help you find punctuation errors, possible grammatical errors, and even improper word choices.

- Above all, edit numerous times, proofread numerous times, and have someone else look over the writing for errors.

ETHICAL ENCOUNTERS

The supervisor asks you to prepare a speech she can deliver to a community organization. You decide to use a few ideas from an article you've read. Your deadline is approaching, and you don't have time to go find the internal citation that should go with the thought, so you simply omit it. What are the possible consequences?

It always pays to review your written work prior to sending it or handing it to a colleague or client. Your writing style and accuracy make an instant impression on the reader. People are confident of your professional writing abilities until you give them evidence that their perception of this basic skill is incorrect.

TYPES OF WRITING IN THE WORKPLACE

There are various forms of writing in corporate life. You can master them quickly as you become more familiar with the requirements of the job.

E-mail

E-mails should be brief. If you find that you are writing a message beyond a screen length, then it is time to pick up the phone and call someone. Always think about the best channel for your message. E-mails are great for scheduling meetings and appointments, following up on issues requiring a brief response, alerting someone to a situation, participating in webinars, etc. An e-mail message is usually brief.

However, e-mails are an easy channel in which to make writing errors. Your typing speed while writing, responding, and sending messages makes this form of communication extremely vulnerable to spelling and grammatical errors. Many e-mail programs don't spell-check well. If you consider yourself a poor speller, we suggest you write your e-mail message in a word processing program first (and remember that spell-check is only one tool, not a panacea), and then cut and paste the message into your e-mail. While this extra step will add a few seconds to your response time, it is worth the effort for the message to be accurate. As an aside, timely responses are a definite plus, but it is also sometimes a good idea to take some time to compose an appropriate response. Rather than hitting "reply" (or "reply all") immediately and not reflecting on what you want to say—especially if the subject is uncomfortable for any of the parties involved—take some time to think about your response and to make sure it is accurate in both content and composition.

Emotional reactions to particular words can occasionally overtake you while reading e-mail. Consider what could happen if you were in a bad mood when you opened a critical e-mail. Your mood could influence your perception of the tone of the message. It's an easy mistake to make, which is why you should read every e-mail you receive with an open mind and apply the same standard of mental discipline and clarity to your written response as you do to analyzing the message. Since paralanguage is missing in the written word, we often read our own emotional state into the words before us. Returning to our example of reading an e-mail when you are in a bad mood, what is your first response? Many of us start typing a reply without thinking—we are simply reacting. It is crucial that employees stop, think, and save difficult e-mails until they have time to settle down. Your communication needs to be thoughtful and professional at all times. Move the e-mail to a folder and reply later. If it helps "blow off steam," draft a reply but make certain you do not send it.

It is best to set difficult correspondence aside briefly prior to responding. Wait a few minutes, hours, or a day if you can. Then, go back and read the original e-mail again. Occasionally you may want someone else to help you interpret an e-mail for legal reasons prior to your response. There is nothing wrong in seeking clarity for any message rather than making a mistake. See if a colleague perceives the same tone as you do in the material. If you drafted an initial response, can you reword it? What are the consequences of sending what you wrote? It is useful to anticipate a response to your words before you send them rather than after they are sent.

E-mail can also create an ethical dilemma. Once in a while people do not pay attention to the contact list on correspondence. You could receive information not intended for you because the sender hits "all" rather than "reply." This is another extremely difficult situation to handle professionally because you are now aware of information not intended for you. As awkward as it is to receive unintended e-mail, it is perhaps worse to send it. Not paying attention to detail can affect your personal credibility tremendously, as happened to the woman who received a general announcement note sent to numerous employees from a friend in the company and decided to tell her about a date she had the previous night. She mistakenly hit the "reply all" button instead of the "reply" button, and the details of her juicy date went to every coworker in the division. This situation sounds slightly absurd, but some employees mistakenly divulge personal information or thoughts via corporate technology during working hours, and this was, indeed, a real situation. It shouldn't happen, but it does. In other words, business communication decisions are not as simple as they might appear to be.

"Thank-you" Notes

Thank-you notes are a terrific way to stand out in your business life and personal life. Many people no longer bother sending a thank-you note for anything. While an electronic thank-you note may be socially acceptable for many today, they are far less personal than a handwritten note. If your handwriting is not legible, you may need to practice cursive writing to improve your skill. Sometimes choosing a script word processing font, printing the note, and tracing a few times can help you learn the cursive style required. A handwritten note says that you took additional personal time to demonstrate your gratitude to someone for thoughtfulness. Since so few individuals use handwritten notes anymore, your effort is likely to impress the receiver.

Invitations

You should print invitations if they are formal, or you can create them through e-mail or electronic services such as Evite if they are casual. Electronic invitations are gradually becoming an acceptable social practice for the technological generation. However, invitations should always include the purpose, date, day, time, and place at the very least. For example:

All Employees

are invited to join in a celebration
for the retirement of

John Jones

Friday, Dec. 6, 2014 at 4:00 p.m.
in the North Board Room

Many people make the mistake of only giving the numerical date on an invitation and not the day of the week. This means that recipients have to take the time to look up the day of the week to determine whether or not they can attend. Occasionally people respond positively to an invitation without noticing a previous conflict because they respond to the date rather than the day of the week for the event. Stating the day is a simple way to reinforce the timing of your event so that people can respond accurately.

Letters

Employees generally print business letters on corporate letterhead, which instantly creates a legal document. Your company probably has a template you can use for correspondence, or you may need to construct your own format in some cases. The format of business letters has changed over the years. Today, most business sites recommend using the flush left block format. According to Purdue's online writing lab, business letters consist of the following (OWL, n.d.):

- the date

- your address (we add our e-mail as well—in today's world, that is the most common contact)

- the person and address you are writing to

April 1, 2014

112 Allen
Department of Communication and Theatre
Mansfield University
Mansfield, PA 16933
kyoung@mansfield.edu

Penelope Longfellow, President
Early Retirement Planning, Inc.
345 Water Street
Anytown, PA 16901

Dear President Longfellow:

I would like to discuss my current financial planning with you to make sure I am doing everything I can to have a stable retirement. There are a couple of future dates that I am considering for retirement, and your advice would be extremely helpful. My daily schedule is open after 1:00 p.m. so you can select a meeting time at your convenience. I have listed my e-mail address above. I look forward to hearing from you.

(If I had more to say, my second paragraph would start here and have spacing before and after it.)

Sincerely,

Kathryn Sue Young

Kathryn Sue Young

- salutation ("Dear Mr./Mrs." or "To Whom it May Concern" followed by a colon)

- the paragraphs of the letter

- a closing ("Sincerely" or "Regards" followed by a comma)

- your name

- type the word "enclosures" if you have included other documents

Note that there are spaces between the sections above. You will need four lines of space between your closing and your typed name so that you have enough room to sign your name. We recommend a pen with black ink for your signature because it can be photocopied; blue ink often does not photocopy well.

Memo Writing

Employees use a memo to make an announcement, remind colleagues of an event or policy change, report the results of a meeting, or share other information. Memos typically contain four parts: (1) the person to whom the memo is addressed, (2) the person from whom it was sent, (3) what it is about (this is labeled RE: or Subject), and (4) the date. Be sure to put your initials immediately after your name. You don't sign a memo, but you should initial it. A basic memo looks like this:

Kathryn Sue Young and Associates

MEMO

To: All Employees

From: Kathryn Sue Young   *KSY*

RE: New Door Locking Policy

Date: April 15, 2010

EFFECTIVE IMMEDIATELY

Effective immediately, all employees must lock all doors when no one is present as you leave. We have received a number of reports of office theft in the building recently, and we ask each employee to lock your office door when leaving, even if you plan to be back momentarily. We appreciate your cooperation.

Most companies have a memo template as part of their corporate software package. This electronic convenience ensures that all internal and external memos have the same "look." You should only have to type the content of a memo onto the template prior to sending it.

There will be times when you feel it necessary to write a "self-protective" memo (also known by more colorful terms!). You would write one of these memos any time you determined it would be wise to possess a paper-trail of a specific event. I (KSY) can still remember the first such memo I had to write. I was a graduate student teaching oral communication at Penn State University, and one of my students gave a speech on three ways to kill someone. It was unsettling, unnerving, and downright creepy. In this instance, it was important for me to let my supervisor know that something unusual had happened. I wrote a memo documenting what had happened and who was involved and sent it to my supervisor for his information.

The self-protective paper-trail memo is also useful when the content of a meeting at which you are present sounds questionable. Although you may not be able to say anything about a statement or policy when it's made, you can certainly send a simple clarification note to the person who presented the idea. You may not receive a response from the person but your note has a date and time code which may be useful later should the communicator be challenged legally or try to blame you for the situation. A memo or note of this type is usually a personal decision and discussed with no one. Your note of clarification is for your records only, and you typically remove a copy of it from the work site and store in a safe place just in case you need it at a future date.

Formal Task Report

Your employer may ask you to join a task group to solve a problem. Once you are finished, you typically turn in a report of your findings plus the group's recommendations for solving it.

As you write this report, your strategy is important (Young, Wood, Phillips, and Pedersen, 2007). Many groups simply divide information-gathering tasks, and each group member writes a section of the report. Your group should be aware that there are many problems inherent with this strategy. First, the writing skills of group members usually vary. You don't want some sections to be written well and others to be confusing. Second, each person has his/her own writing style. When a manager reads the entire report, those stylistic shifts can quickly become annoying and distracting. Third, occasionally group members do not do their work. If a group member does not finish his/her section, then the rest of the group is required to complete that section to meet a deadline. Finally, if using the individually written section strategy, the report will require extensive editing to correct errors and to achieve a readable flow. Unfortunately, most groups are pressed for time at the end of a project. In this situation, there is a tendency to rush the written report, which produces substandard results. You don't want this to happen after working for a long time on a project. Therefore, it is useful to plan a time line for the entire writing process within the team.

ETHICAL ENCOUNTERS

The CEO praises your boss at the annual meeting for his report on proposed changes in your division. However, you wrote the cited report. It becomes evident that your boss removed your name and put her own on it. What do you do?

As one writer completes the rough draft, another person can begin the initial editing. Having two or three people involved in multiple revisions almost always guarantees a tighter, more professional report. After your group completes the report (and time permits), ask another colleague, who is not in the group, to proofread the document for errors or unclear wording.

This may sound like a lot of work—it is. If you became accustomed to turning in first drafts of your writing in school, then it is time to break the habit as you begin a working career. We have seen too many groups who put numerous hours of work into their problem-solving projects only to hand in a sloppy draft as their final report. That last-minute error in judgment destroys all of the group's hard work. The presentation of your written work either enhances or diminishes your professional credibility. It's essential to save enough time and effort to execute this portion of the task well.

ETHICAL ENCOUNTERS

You take a colleague's ideas and present them in a report as your own. What are the potential consequences?

As you begin your report draft, there are a number of sections that may be useful to consider for inclusion (Young et al., 2007). They include:

- A title page
- An executive summary
- Background of the problem
- Explanation of the criteria
- Explanation of the best solution and how it meets the criteria
- Presentation of the plan
- Argued defense
- Conclusion

Title page.   You should include a title page with any professional formatted report:

- Title
- Group name or title of task force (if appropriate)
- Members' names
- Date
- Name of person receiving the report

Executive summary.   The executive summary usually contains:

- A statement of the task
- A review of the problem-solving process
- The routing for the final report (who gets it)
- A preview of the proposal
- Acknowledgments (if appropriate)

Don't try to say too much in the executive summary. This should be a brief summary of the task. Your group may want to detail what it went through. Remember that *no one rewards you for the effort you made; you are rewarded only for the effectiveness of your final product.* Pay attention to the needs of the receiver who reads the report rather than justifying your own hard work. Your employer will judge your group by the results. The hours spent in meetings and doing research is only part of the task. Make sure to spend the time necessary to present a report worthy of a positive impression after all the group's hard work.

Consider your audience carefully, though. If they are hostile to your plan, you may need to present solid evidence to build the problem before you preview its solution. Your group will have to decide whether to include this evidence in the executive summary of your final report.

Background. You should include all of the evidence that a problem exists (with appendices as appropriate):

- Detailed description of the problem, supported with evidence including:
  - ✓ Statistics
  - ✓ Research
  - ✓ Expert and personal testimony
  - ✓ Examples and illustrations
- Discussion of possible causes, supported with evidence
- Explanation of whether your group will deal with symptoms and/or causes
- Projection of what might happen if the problem is not addressed or need is not met

By the time the reader finishes reading this section, he/she should truly understand every facet of the problem.

Criteria. You should include the following in this section:

- Explain your criteria
- Define any terms
- Explain the order of importance of criteria

Presentation of the plan. You should present your solution in complete detail (Young et al., 2007). Do not make the mistake of putting too little detail into your plan. If someone else is in charge of approving the plan, they are much more likely to do so if your presentation provides sufficient detail that they can take immediate action. If they have to do a lot of work to figure out the plan's logic, they probably won't make the effort.

Typically, you would include the following:

- Who?
- Does what?
- For what reasons?

- With what resources?

- Under whose supervision?

- At what cost? To be provided by whom?

- Evaluated as follows

Remember that the receiver of the final report has *only* the report on which to base a judgment. If you present an inadequate report, the receiver will assume you are an inadequate group.

The argued defense.   Your group must be prepared to defend its solution against whatever arguments others might make (Young et al., 2007). In most cases, persuasive proposals succeed when the proposal identifies and refutes any arguments the audience may have. In this final step, your group must deal with the question: "What can be done to prepare the most persuasive case possible for acceptance of our proposal?" You should first assess the possible obstacles to adoption:

- Who might speak out against the proposal?

- Who stands to lose?

- Who has offered a different solution about which they might feel defensive?

Be prepared to answer the following attacks:

- There is no need/problem.

- There is a problem, but the plan is unworkable.

- There is a problem and the plan is workable, but it will not solve the problem.

- The plan is needed, workable, and will solve the problem, but it will bring undesirable effects (too costly, violates legal or moral limitations, etc.).

- The reasoning is ineffective. The documentation is ineffective.

Next, it is important to determine what your supervisor wants. Unfortunately, the world is not always a place where honest people do honest work and are rewarded honestly. To make an effective appeal, you will have to look at the personal interests of those who pass judgment. Here are some issues to consider.

- The decision maker may have a sphere of influence. Does your proposal weaken or strengthen his or her influence?

- The decision maker may not be prepared to take on more work. Does your operations plan provide for additional people to reduce the pressure?

- The decision maker may be concerned about how particular individuals are affected by changes. Does your proposal displace anyone? What influence do potentially displaced people have on the decision maker? Can you protect them?

In this section of your report, you should include:

- An assessment of possible obstacles to the adoption of the solution.

- An answer to every possible argument against the solution.

- A final argument restating your solution and how it solves the problem.

Conclusion.   Include any summary material that reinforces your message.

Writing a formal or team report is a test of numerous analytical and writing skills. Each and every time you submit a business report, make sure the final document represents your best work. Just as your writing improves the more you do it, your advancement within an organization improves as colleagues consistently receive quality work from you.

TECHNOLOGY AND THE WORKPLACE

Perhaps generational differences are most evident in one's familiarity with technology. Today, four generations (those who lived through World War II, Baby Boomers, GenX, and Millennials) work together. Digital natives grew up with the Internet, while previous generations have had to adapt to technological changes. Technology in the workplace brings new challenges for communication in part due to the speed at which decisions are made. You need to master each piece of new technology as it is made available to you by your employer. While the Millennials and the generation after them were raised with digital games and computers requiring accuracy using physical and visual speed, the modern workplace adds thinking, analyzing material, and writing to the communication mix.

PowerPoint

If you are creating a PowerPoint presentation, you want to be as professional as possible. You need to present materials clearly with the audience in mind rather than using inappropriate production tricks that diffuse your message. PowerPoint should always be informative and visually appealing rather than gimmicky and entertaining. As you design your slides, make sure not to exceed six words per line or six lines per slide. Also make sure that your letter color is in high contrast to your background color and use the same background for each slide.

Web Conferencing

Computer-based meetings give you the opportunity to share written information throughout a discussion. Whether you are typing questions for general discussion, analyzing data as it is presented, e-mailing, developing slides during a discussion, etc., the material you generate is shared immediately with colleagues throughout the company who are participating in the discussion. Avoiding writing errors during this real-time experience will highlight your professionalism.

Electronic Document Preparation

Free web-based software applications are available to large/small businesses, schools, community groups, and nonprofit organizations. The applications allow users to create and edit documents in "real" time. Two services to check out are Google Docs and Wikis.

Google Docs allows you to import, create, edit, and update documents in various file formats—combining text with formulas, lists, tables, and images. Most word processing programs and presentation software work on Google Docs. The finished product can be published as a Web page or as a manuscript. Users can control who sees their work.

Wikis also allows users to collaborate with each other quite easily. Google Docs and Wikis give individuals working together on a project the ability to contribute their ideas and writing skills to a document from any geographic location. Documents become more collaborative and collegial as participants use their creativity and editing skills to create a unified document prior to its release for management, clients, or the public. Because every member working on a project can perfect the final outcome, the completed document should have solid content, editing, and writing. Documents can come together faster when teams/employees can access the project around the clock on their computers.

No individual working on a project using this technology can say he or she was left out of the process. Like all digital communication, however, a business's major concern is information security. Internal and external projects should only be read/seen by those individuals for whom they were designed.

Social Networking

Historically, self-disclosure was primarily limited to face-to-face interpersonal communication. Today, millions of people self-disclose via the Internet to a multitude of unknown receivers. Through MySpace, Facebook, Twitter, discussion boards, blogs and texting, people are posting personal facts about themselves that were once reserved for close, life-long friends. New media is shifting the traditional role of self-disclosure in interpersonal communication.

If there are people we want to research/track, we can quickly find them through the Internet and discover their hopes, dreams, favorite movies, foods, songs, social activities, home address, pictures, etc. All of these insights into their character are posted by the people themselves without privacy concerns. On many social-networking sites, a stranger can discover personal information about a colleague that traditionally would never be mentioned or revealed throughout a lifetime of working together as colleagues. Your digital footprint needs to be examined to make sure you don't mind if business associates become aware of your background.

The interview process today increasingly includes checking publically available databases like Facebook. A recent graduate reported that she was told to pull up her MySpace site during a job interview. Fortunately for her, there was nothing compromising on her site. We find, however, that most of our students aren't so prudent. Many of our students post pictures of questionable behavior, poses, and attire; list

ETHICAL ENCOUNTERS

What do you do when your colleagues want to friend you, but you want to keep your personal life private and separate from work? Do you have an ethical obligation to friend a boss or colleague if they ask through a social-networking site? What if you want to keep your personal life separate from your work life? If you say yes, what ethical considerations will you need to consider with every future status update on social networking?

membership in groups that reveal a lot about their moral character; and use profanity, demeaning, and derogatory language in their posts. There have been many debates about privacy issues and the ethics of checking personal information via these sites, but the fact remains that employers have access to a significant amount of information about you.

Benefits.   Certainly, self-disclosing via technology can be used for good purposes. For example, I (KSY) keep track of the accomplishments and career moves of former students through the use of Facebook. The technology gives me the opportunity to see how their education has benefited them throughout their lives. However, I also choose to post very limited information about myself.

Dangers.   There are negative aspects to social networking as well. People often mistakenly assume they are anonymous when they visit websites online, but every movement can be collected in a database. Twitter ushered in what some have called "thoughtcasting"—encouraging people to erase the barrier between private thought and public expression (Croal, 2008). If your job is listed on Salary.com and your vacation preferences on Orbitz, both might affect your ability to negotiate a raise or apply for a loan. Credit-card companies use social media to determine what advertisements will be most effective for a social group or to determine if someone is likely to default on a loan (Bennett, 2010). An insurance company discontinued sick leave benefits for a woman in Quebec after they found photos of her on Facebook that contradicted her stated medical condition. Even the IRS scours social-networking sites for people bragging about cheating on their taxes. Nothing is safe to reveal.

Employers can check your Facebook page to see if you really missed work because you claimed you were ill. It would be easy for human resources to review the sites of employees periodically to see what colleagues are doing when they are out for an illness as well as to make sure they represent the company in a professional manner. This constant scrutiny of personal information may seem unreasonable, but it is available. Scrutiny of a person's character could affect future bonuses, promotions, and continuation of employment. As these examples demonstrate, the interplay of technology, self-disclosure, and interpersonal communication in the workplace is complicated. The technical revolution in communication means coworkers, teachers, law enforcement, family members, and religious acquaintances can assess your information instantly and make judgments about your character.

Have you ever made comments on a blog or written an e-mail using language and expressions you would never use in person? Steve Johnson, a critic for the *Chicago Tribune*, says "nothing exposes what lurks in the dark corners of our souls more effectively than a keyboard and the firewall of physical remove from whomever you're writing to or about" (Johnson, 2008). We recently read about someone who was fired from his job because the daughter of the employer read comments made about her father on a website of a young woman who was venting about how the boss was a jerk and kept her father at work so he couldn't attend her school event. The two daughters attended the same school. Freedom of interpersonal expression can have disastrous consequences. Technology and our willingness to use it open doors to multiple avenues of checking our credibility and social interactions while not at work.

Guidelines.   There are some general guidelines to follow to help safeguard your reputation. Establish privacy settings so your posts on social-networking sites aren't accessible to the general public. In addition, assume that all communication might become public. Don't use offensive language or refer to illegal behaviors on your sites. Do not post about work and colleagues on your social-networking sites, and never visit those sites on company time unless it is required for your job. It is usually safe to assume that you can do personal business on technology that you own and during your own time. However if the company gives you a handheld device for communication as part of your job, it is best to only conduct business on that device.

Some employees appear to be tied to their mobile technology like a doctor "on call." However, other employees do not have this connection to the employer because their position does not require constant connection to the company or they simply choose to ignore work when they aren't there. Familiarize yourself with company policy about technology and when you are expected to be available.

Sam Ladner (2008) states, "The use of mobile technology does indeed break down the home/work division, but their use alone does not necessarily result in this breakdown. Rather, it is the underlying social relations of workplaces that affect how individuals negotiate the use of these technologies in non-work time and space" (p. 466).

FINAL THOUGHTS

Solid writing remains a critical skill for employment and professional advancement; business writing must be logical and factual—and inviting to read. Many people think they won't write as much when they leave school; the reality is, they write more. The days of not paying attention to editing your work and how you express yourself end with employment. Your ability to express yourself clearly and concisely becomes a reflection of a company's credibility. You are a public relations vehicle for your employer at work and in the community. Companies notice individuals with effective written and verbal skills.

New technologies use different jargon to communicate rapidly with receivers. It will be necessary to adjust to the various written styles required by specific technologies and to the culture of the receiver. Multitasking is a required skill. You may be web conferencing with colleagues on different continents, e-mailing, and editing the report on a Wiki.

The audience for your writing can be national or international—in addition to being legally binding as a representative of the corporation. Read everything carefully and repeatedly to make sure you have stated your facts and thoughts clearly and informatively.

KEY TERMS

E-mail	Nonverbal message
Formal task reports	PowerPoint
Invitations	Thank-you notes
Letters	Web conferencing
Memo writing	Writing skills

EXERCISES

1. Discuss your strengths and weaknesses when it comes to writing. How do you plan to improve weak areas?

2. Write a thank-you note in cursive.

3. Develop a PowerPoint sales pitch for using web conferencing.

4. Write a letter to your teacher stating why you deserve a good grade for the course.

5. Exchange your résumé with classmates and critique one another.

6. Bring an e-mail you've written to class. Exchange the e-mail with another student looking for advice on how to be a more effective communicator.

7. Write an invitation for a special event.

Teamwork and Your Career

GOALS

After reading this chapter you should be able to:

✓ Distinguish between groups and teams

✓ Identify what new groups should do to get started

✓ Compare and contrast task and social elements of group work

✓ Differentiate among different types of followers

✓ Effectively plan and run meetings

✓ Participate in a virtual meeting

Many self-motivated individuals find it difficult to work in groups/ teams. And yet, corporate organizational patterns often require employees to work together to solve problems and accomplish goals on a daily basis. It is important to recognize that colleagues—whose background and work experiences are unique—will bring valuable insights to numerous projects. Merging various personalities and skills in a cohesive working environment is critical for a successful business and for employee morale. We build trust incrementally with each day of working together. You gain trust in colleagues' skills and their execution of those skills as you observe their work and behavior over time—just as they will learn to trust you. An open mind when working with others combined with a personal commitment to excellence will help you become a valued team member.

DISTINGUISHING BETWEEN GROUPS AND TEAMS

Groups are composed of individuals with similar ideas or goals who come together to complete a task or solve a problem for a common organizational good. A sense of cohesiveness while working together distinguishes a team from a standard work group. **Teams** begin with colleagues or strangers who develop interpersonal skills and task responsibilities quickly. A team becomes cohesive as members work to accomplish their task. This cohesiveness can be seen and felt by colleagues who aren't even part of the team. There are many facets to good team problem solving because you must work on a task while simultaneously dealing with the intricacies of interpersonal differences. Only when you blend effective task work with effective interpersonal skills do you have an ideally functioning team.

There are many task groups in the workplace in which people don't feel a sense of belonging, don't support a common goal, and don't worry about their interactions with each other. This is not a team. Some corporations use the team concept in the workplace successfully. By using the word "teams," corporations encourage a spirit of family, cohesiveness, and productivity. However, some corporations promoting the team philosophy still do not achieve their goal. Many employees never actively contribute to this spirit even though they do their work. Everyone must fully cooperate with other members throughout the duration of a task to achieve the team label. Forming a team is an ideal goal for any small group working on a task, but personalities sometimes block cohesion.

AN EFFECTIVE BEGINNING

So how do you become a team member? The first few minutes of interacting with a new group of people present the same challenges as a first impression in an interpersonal relationship. Colleagues may like or dislike each other based on their appearance, nonverbals, or preconceived notions about each other's work based on previous experiences. The group must become cohesive quickly and forget their personal differences in order to be effective and complete the assigned task. Bosses have little tolerance for pettiness between group members.

For example, in your fifth week you are assigned to a task force to review the current policy statement, "No personal business may be conducted during work hours," and make a recommendation for modification or continuation of the existing policy. You learn that Anthony, Nancy, Rafael, Sheng, and Lenora have also been assigned to the task force. You are disappointed to discover that Anthony is in your group. He didn't complete expected tasks on time when you worked with him on an earlier assignment. You've also noticed that he usually arrives at work late and leaves early. Even when Anthony is in the office, he is obstinate and argumentative. You are not looking forward to dealing with him as a member of the task force. You are somewhat thankful, however, that Lenora is in your group, since she expresses her opinions in a positive way and is passionate about her work.

You meet with your colleagues for the first time. Theoretically, a new group should do the following:

- Introduce one another
- Assess everyone's skills
- Assess everyone's goals
- Assess everyone's needs

Introductions

Take a minute to introduce people. There are many times when people don't know one another. If the leader begins with "I think we all know each other…," don't be afraid to introduce yourself to someone you haven't met previously.

Skills

Depending on the task, an initial skills assessment might be necessary to determine who is best-suited for the various tasks necessary to complete the project—for example: research, writing, editing, proofreading, critical thinking, and visual and oral presentation. Once you know who can do what, the leader can assign members to the proper tasks. It is obviously self-defeating to randomly assign the final draft to someone who can't write well. Assess member skills immediately and quickly so the project can move forward.

At a practical level, however, most business groups skip these steps. When people have worked together a long time, they already know each individual's strengths. If you are the only one new to the group, volunteer information about your skills if no one asks. Your reputation is important, so get assigned to a project that aligns with your skills.

ETHICAL ENCOUNTERS

What are the ethical considerations of telling the group that you are strong at something when you really are weak?

Goals

All group members should reach a common understanding of the goals of each member. What does each person want out of the experience? An initial conversation about goals can save a lot of misunderstandings and hard feelings later. Sometimes we work on exciting projects, and everyone is committed to doing their best. Other times, the task may be "busywork"—everyone knows no one will ever look at their work and evaluate it. In that case, you may decide just to get the task done and not put a lot of effort into it. The clearer the members are about their goals, the more cohesive the group will be and the closer they will be to ideal team status. In our example about personal business during working hours, the team knows that whatever policy they devise becomes the new working policy within the department.

Doing a basic inventory of members' skills is a good start, but it does not guarantee success. If a colleague fails to follow through with a commitment, his or her strengths become irrelevant. In your first meeting, everyone's commitment to the project is usually pretty high. But as time passes and other deadlines get in the way, you may see some colleagues skip meetings, come unprepared, or behave in a disinterested, harried, or belligerent manner during the meeting. Achieving maximum effort from each member is essential to building cohesiveness.

Members' Needs

Colleagues work together to accomplish tasks daily. Many managers allow employees or coworkers to function as a group on various projects. In order for employees to morph into a team, additional interpersonal efforts need to happen. One of the ways to get people feeling as though they are a part of team is to inquire about and accommodate their individual needs. For example, one member might need advance notice for meetings and assignments; another does best with positive feedback; another looks for praise for good work.

Sometimes finding out what people need is as simple as asking a question in the break room. "Hey Sam, what did you find to be the most aggravating thing in your last committee?" or "Hi Laura, I'm running this group and I was wondering if there is anything you were hoping the new chair would do?"

Many managers don't bother to ascertain why employees don't seem to have "passion" for their job and the company. Some supervisors feel that you are there to do a job, so just do it. They don't care if you need advance notice—you'll get it when you get it. They don't care if you are motivated by praise, and they won't give it. They may sense employee morale is low, but they ignore it if the work gets done. It is extremely difficult to establish the concept of teamwork in an office without good morale. Poor morale makes everyone's experience a miserable one. Leadership influences morale, which is discussed in chapter 8.

Typically, a group becomes a team when it is cohesive and enthusiastically tackles assignments with equal passion. Team members feel they are a part of something valuable and possibly special. They are happy to be working with their colleagues. Do colleagues always agree? No. Is there occasional conflict? Yes. But everyone knows at the end of their time together that morale is high, and they've been working with other people who value their contributions. They've created a great outcome: new policy, report, restructuring scheme, and so on.

Responsible managers consider, talk about, and analyze each employee's needs to facilitate solid teamwork. It's easier to work interpersonally with colleagues when you understand one another. Some people need a lot of encouragement; they need to hear people say they are doing a good job occasionally. Other people are self-directed and find comments like "good idea!" to be condescending. Some people need to be in charge. Others have a high need for organization. And others may simply want to goof off. The more you know about people's needs, the better you can communicate with them. If every group member chooses to interact effectively on an interpersonal level, your group will be well on the way toward a team feeling where personal motivation and morale remains high.

Another factor to consider in deciding whether to assess member needs is the amount of time available for the assigned task. If you are getting together to review a policy statement, you'll be done in a meeting or two. You are going to meet, discuss changes in the language of the policy, and make a recommendation. On the other hand, if you are part of a public relations team developing a campaign for a new client, or you are in a group charged with determining how to expand your business, reaching a workable solution will take time. In these situations, communication is more effective when members consider colleagues' needs throughout the project to fully comprehend verbal and nonverbal exchanges. You can reach team status more rapidly when a colleague's needs are respected and valued.

Motivation can come in many forms. Some people are internally motivated. A break in routine, getting some food, or the comments of team members motivate others. It is important for team members to discuss motivational ideas and decide what methods might work for everyone. Those colleagues who think they are already motivated and won't benefit from this discussion are fooling themselves. Teams can lack motivation to move forward at any point during a project's development and for a variety of reasons. You should revisit the initial discussion regarding motivation whenever the project focus dips. The more people enjoy working together, the better the final report/conclusion is going to be.

TASK VERSUS SOCIAL ELEMENTS OF TEAMWORK

As you begin any project, it is important to remember that teamwork involves task elements and social elements. **Task elements** relate directly to the project itself—setting up meetings, collecting research and analyzing it, and writing a final report. **Social elements** include the entire interpersonal experience—chatting with one another, asking if people are doing well, and joking around when appropriate. Some people are very social all of the time, and nothing gets accomplished. Other people are so task oriented they prefer to begin working as soon as they enter the room. They call the group to order immediately, get to the business of the day, and become annoyed when someone cracks a joke. Neither of these methods works well. In order to work effectively on a team, you need to have a reasonable mix of task and social elements.

In most group work environments, it makes sense to spend a little time initially working with social elements. There should be a brief time, maybe even five minutes, where people can say hello, talk about the latest news, tell a joke, gripe about something going on, or simply make some observations that are not work related. But the group should remember that once the initial greeting period is complete, the meeting will be called to order, and everyone gets down to the business agenda. Even though this traditional interpersonal method of working with others is quickly shifting to technology, including meetings conducted on your personal computing device, this initial greeting period is still important.

If the work session becomes intense, it may be useful to build a "time out" break into the meeting structure. The value of scheduled breaks and possible comic relief by some team members can assist the team in maintaining focus when discussions become intense or if a meeting runs longer than planned. A little laughter or off-target commentary sometimes provides needed stress relief. After the "time out," the business conversation continues.

As specific tasks (taking notes, research, analyzing data, etc.) are assigned to various team members, and you volunteer to do additional tasks during the meeting, your follow through is critical if you want to maintain personal credibility. We have worked with many colleagues who say that they will have answers to questions e-mailed to us by a certain time, only to check the computer for the information and discover it isn't there. You must deliver information to people who are counting on you by the time set for its delivery. Supervisors notice your ability to get things completed on time, and the behavior will usually be rewarded with future advancement, a bonus, or retaining your position during a time of restructuring.

ETHICAL ENCOUNTERS

A team member does not meet a deadline. You panic as team leader and begin to do the member's share of the work without informing the person of your decision. Should you contact your colleague to find out what is going on? Ignore the missed deadline completely? Rally other colleagues behind you and against the rogue team member? File a final report dropping the team member's name from the title page?

Teamwork can often be problematic. It takes skill and patience to solve problems and integrate personalities into a cohesive team. There are occasions when it will seem more difficult to accomplish a task by working in a group instead of working on your own. However, at many points in your career you will have to work in a group. Learn the necessary skills to have a good team experience. Once you make effective choices and are committed to a team and the task, you should have a solid, rewarding experience.

In order to be successful as a team, you must find ways to trust, to encourage, and to motivate each other. Your interpersonal skills can make the difference between a successful team experience and a poor team experience.

FOLLOWERSHIP— THE EMPLOYEE'S ROLE

A tremendous challenge to any new employee is to sort out which colleagues possess real passion and talent for their jobs. These individuals can usually inspire you to learn faster and work harder to achieve their level of happiness within corporate life. Not all employees are motivated, however, and you need to navigate your way around these individuals until you can determine why people do and say the things they do. Positive behavior will be valued; negative behavior adversely affects your reputation and possibly your employment. It is important to be a good listener and observer of the business environment as you start your career and throughout your professional life. Treat colleagues with respect and maintain a good attitude toward them regardless of how you feel about them personally. Only time will reveal whether your initial perceptions of others are accurate.

Robert Kelley (1992) encourages followers (as well as leaders) to understand their communication styles in order to be effective. His research revealed that followers differ on two dimensions: (1) independent/critical thinking and (2) active engagement. The best **followers** are those who think for themselves and initiate action (Hackman and Johnson, 2009). Typical followers take direction and complete jobs after being told what is expected of them. The worst followers need constant supervision. So until you get a leadership position, what kind of follower do you want to be? How will you deal with other followers who do not share your positive goals?

Michael Hackman and Craig Johnson (2009) summarize the five categories of followers identified by Kelley.

- *Alienated followers* are disillusioned with leaders; they use their independent thinking to fight rather than to serve organizations.
- *Conformists* defer to authority; although committed to the organization, they rarely express their opinions.
- *Pragmatists* are moderately independent and engaged.
- *Passive followers* rely on direction and meet only minimal expectations.
- *Exemplary followers* are active, innovative, think critically, and exceed requirements.

Learning the skills possessed by exemplary followers allows others to reach the same level of success.

Exemplary followers understand what is important in helping the organization reach its objectives and develop the skills required. They network throughout the organization by joining teams, reaching out to others in the organization, and working with leaders as partners. They anticipate ethical problems and work through issues that could pose a significant threat and put the organization at risk.

Ira Chaleff talks about courage—accepting a higher level of risk—as an important characteristic of followers. Being courageous is easier if followers remember that their allegiance is to the corporation rather than to the leader (Hackman and Johnson, 2009). Chaleff (2009) addresses six areas of courage for followers and one for leaders. Followers should develop the courage to:

- Assume responsibility (to be accountable, to assess skills and attitudes, seek feedback)

- Serve (be organized, develop time-management skills, exercise good judgment, meet/exceed expectations)

- Challenge (ask questions, provide feedback, avoid groupthink, address abuses)

- Participate in transformation (control reactions to confrontation, create supportive environment, model empathy)

- Take moral action (disobey unethical directives, threaten to resign)

- Speak to the hierarchy (be prepared, educate others, speak up, be patient and persistent)

Leaders should develop the courage to listen to followers (invite creative challenges, accept support and criticism, develop a culture of communication).

Barbara Kellerman (2008) offers another characterization of followers in an organization. Analyze the varying approaches. You will find a great deal of information that will help you hone your skills in analyzing each situation.

- *Isolates* are completely detached. These followers are scarcely aware of what's going on. They don't care about, know about, or respond to their leaders in any way. Because of this, they passively support the status quo. They are most likely to be found in large companies where they can get away with acting this way.

- *Bystanders* observe but do not participate. These followers are free riders who deliberately stand aside and disengage from leaders as well as other members of the organization. They are perfectly aware of what is going on around them; they just choose not to take part in any of it.

- *Participants* are engaged in some way. These followers are interested enough to invest something (time or money usually) in their company, but not interested enough to go any further than that.

- *Activists* feel strongly one way or the other about their leaders and organizations and they act accordingly. These followers are eager, energetic, and engaged. They are heavily interested in people as well as processes, so they will work hard to either support or overturn their leaders depending on the situation.

- *Diehards* are prepared to go down for the cause—whether it's an individual, an idea, or both. These followers are either deeply devoted to or against their leader. They are rare and usually emerge in dire (or close to dire) situations.

Think about each of the styles discussed above. Chances are you have worked with all of them at one time or another or will encounter them during your career. In most organizations, there is a mix of these types of followers. If you are fortunate, your group/team experience will include a few of the supportive types to balance the others. But don't fool yourself into believing that when you get into the business world, everyone will be devoted to the company and share your passion for success. You'll find the same mix of people that you are experiencing right now in your classrooms.

There are many dimensions of followership. Some followers are primarily concerned with completing tasks while others focus on maintaining relationships. Different goals require different attributes. The follower styles you encounter will probably reflect the behaviors "expected, demanded, promoted, or discouraged by formal leaders" (Hackman and Johnson, 2009, p. 61). Some followers will work effectively in almost any situation with any leader, but the effectiveness of most followers will depend on the leader.

Your challenge in looking into the future is to determine the type of employee (follower) you want to be. Most workers are a combination of the various categories discussed above. It's a good idea as you start your career to determine how you want to be perceived by other people. Enthusiasm is the best way to make an impression and be remembered by everyone. It takes many years of devotion and hard work to advance to the top within an organization. Therefore, you remain a follower for a long time because someone above you determines your fate. To be a good employee takes patience, passion for business and people, and the constant professional development of your communication skills.

INTERPERSONAL SKILLS IN TEAMS

Excellent interpersonal communication skills are the key to having others perceive you as a valuable team member. How you articulate a message verbally and in writing consistently demonstrates to others your credibility and professionalism. The statements you make reveal your thoughtfulness, analytical ability, research ability, and comprehensive approach to completing a task well. Listen carefully to everything team members say. Think critically about the statements you hear; analyze them for accuracy.

Members of the team will examine your nonverbal reactions to the statements of others. Colleagues perceive you to be a professional by how you react to statements, jokes, memos, e-mails, and general conversation. Someone is always looking at you to see if they can trust you or want to deal with you. You need to appear comfortable even when a conversation or action makes you uneasy. Your reaction to stressful situations can demonstrate ease and sophistication. Maintaining professional conduct at all times is essential.

Multitasking is a requirement. You need to be organized to save time and avoid mistakes in communication. Team members will expect you to remember issues discussed and actions taken. Immediately file every piece of information from team meetings—whether physically or electronically. You must be able to access information easily without wasting time—and especially not the time of other members.

Good team members will analyze all actions in terms of the goals of the organization. Loyal employees use supportive language and behavior to reinforce the mission of the organization. An employee must assess various situations accurately and find the proper words to explain actions and policies. Audience analysis determines how you shape your communication. A closed meeting with colleagues provides greater freedom for raising challenges to proposed procedures than a discussion on the same topic in a community setting. A personal commitment to reshape communication to meet professional demands reflects your passion for a career.

How you want colleagues to perceive your communication skills is within your control. You need to constantly improve your "value" to an employer, and you can do it quite easily by working to sound and look professional. While this may seem like a simple concept, it is not. The components of professionalism are endless—every action you make, your appearance, your sound, your verbal and written communication, your interpersonal skills, the efficient use of time, digital skills, perceived intelligence, perceived leadership potential, perceived responsibility, and multitasking ability.

PLANNING AND RUNNING MEETINGS

Much of a team's work is carried out in meetings when members develop strategy and coordinate assignments. Although such meetings are an everyday occurrence in the business world, you cannot take them lightly. We have all been the victim of a poorly run meeting. Preparation is key to your effective participation in team meetings.

Planning for Meetings

Planning is part of effective teamwork. One team member will be assigned the responsibility for coordinating the details for the meeting site in a conventional setting. In selecting a space, make sure it contains the technology your team needs. For instance, everyone should be comfortable in the meeting space. There should be space to set materials and equipment—a large table that allows you to display/arrange information for the meeting. You need to make sure the lighting is sufficient for everyone attending the meeting. Don't forget record keeping as you make these plans. It may be useful to have an alternative corporate site available to your team just in case the room you have reserved becomes unavailable.

As an individual member, make sure you are 100 percent prepared for whatever is on the agenda. You should have read the minutes of the previous meeting, so you can identify corrections and can vote to approve them. You should have reviewed the agenda, so you know the plan. Be sure you are prepared with a concise, accurate report for your portion of the task. You also need to have completed all of your tasks. Team members get irritated quickly when individuals make excuses for their incomplete work. This shows great disrespect to your team members. There are often severe consequences for not being prepared in business.

Keeping Proper Records

How do you keep proper records? Most groups start with a meeting agenda. The agenda can be formal or informal, depending on the team. Most agendas include the following items:

- A professional heading
- A start time
- Correction and acceptance of previous minutes
- Announcements
- Reports from team members
- Unfinished business from previous meetings
- New business items
- Ending time for the meeting

Surely, you have attended meetings where a team accomplished nothing. The leader began with "What are we doing today?" and no one remembered what had even been decided in the previous meeting. An effective leader creates an agenda and sticks to it. A leader who is organized, prepared, and unwilling to waste time demonstrates respect for the other team members. If the leader can create, distribute, and stick to an effective agenda, the leader earns every member's respect. You cannot waste time in business. Sticking to an agenda demonstrates respect for everyone's time.

Running Proper Meetings

You should always have a formal record of every decision the team makes. This record is called **minutes**. In order to keep proper records, the secretary of the day should indicate the date, a list of who attended the meeting, what time the meeting was called to order, a notation of every item discussed, who initiated the idea, and what decision was reached. The secretary should also keep a written record of every vote taken, unless the leader makes a request not to record it for a specific item. Minutes conclude with the phrase "Respectfully Submitted" and the secretary signs his or her name. If the secretary distributes the minutes electronically, a signed original copy is filed for the record.

ETHICAL ENCOUNTERS

There are times in the workforce when your notes and conversations from a group meeting are considered confidential. You must be careful to adhere to the policy or agreements related to confidentiality that your team or organization establishes. You accidentally leave the notes from a closed meeting on your desk as you head to lunch. When you return, you discover a colleague was in your office to collect some material you had promised to pass along and you think this person read your confidential notes. How should you react to this situation?

Some miscellaneous tips for record keeping include keeping a file folder of all agendas, all copies of the minutes, copies of all e-mail correspondence, copies of all memos, and copies of any handouts from team members. You should also date all information that crosses your desk so you know when you received it. A secretary's goal is to keep all information concerning a specific project in one file.

You write minutes in a formal style, with no abbreviations. Be sure that you spell and record all members' names correctly. In formal business, use only the last name of individuals in the record. Everyone should take responsibility for reviewing and editing minutes prior to voting to approve them. There are many formats for minutes that you can find on the Internet, but businesses usually have a preferred style you should follow.

Meeting Dos and Don'ts

While there is no comprehensive list of what you should and should not do in a group meeting, we offer these suggestions:

- Be on time.
- Stick to the topic and stay on task.
- Leave personal issues behind.
- Be prepared.
- Have handouts ready, if appropriate.
- Give an update of where you are on the project.
- Don't keep a critique to yourself to appear to be popular.
- Be positive when you ask questions of other members.
- Remember the difference between being critical of an idea and criticizing an idea or person.
- Use proper, respectful tone when being critical of an idea.
- Be honest about what you can/can't do.
- Follow through.
- If you are having difficulty, say so as early as possible, so other members can help you.

Virtual Meetings

The need for virtual meetings and virtual teams in business is increasing rapidly. An employee's personal computing device can now serve as a meeting room. Corporations are licensing enterprising software companies like Cisco Systems, Inc., Citrix systems, Microsoft, HP, Google, etc. to provide their information technology (IT) needs rather than maintaining their own IT staff. Companies are still investing and using the latest technologies, but they are hiring outside vendors to provide the programming software features and applications they need, maintenance for the service, server facilities for information storage, as well as security for the information exchanged and stored. Licensing agreements with software providers save corporations money because an external business assumes the financial cost of software development, staff, research and security. These outside software companies provide "cloud computing" or software-as-a-service (SaaS) to anyone who wants (pays for) their services. A "cloud" provides shared resources, software, and information on demand for any user.

For example, Cisco Systems Inc. provides WebEx web conferencing to its clients. It is a secure, interactive, and user-friendly site on which to hold a meeting or conference nationally or internationally. According to the company's website, "WebEx combines real-time desktop sharing with phone conferencing so everyone sees the same thing while you talk. It's far more productive than e-mailing files and struggling to get everyone on the same page over the phone. And it can often eliminate the need for people to travel and meet on site."

Participants can share documents, make visual presentations, and/or demonstrate products and services in a collaborative manner from their desktop. WebEx is a subscription service; there is no software to install, and no hardware to purchase. The licensing fee covers the cost of the service, and it's based on the total number of desktops that have access to the service. Managers can predetermine which employees need which specific features of a software program to perform their job well. Once the distribution specifications are known, the licensing fee can be determined for the corporate package. The personal computer is now the meeting room.

If we can simply flip a switch and meet via computer, we eliminate the time and expense of travel to bring people together. **Virtual teams** consist of dispersed individuals (whether geographically or within an organization) who use information technologies to collaborate and communicate to accomplish a specific goal. Social-networking sites have introduced the under-40 crowd to global discussions on a personal level. The technical preparation of the younger workforce to the exciting possibilities of cultural exchange gives them a definite edge in meeting the demands of modern business. Employers are seeking individuals who are comfortable communicating on digital platforms with a diverse pool of colleagues from multiple cultures. It is also imperative to remember time differences when communicating globally. Sometimes you can communicate during normal working hours; other times, a project may require transmitting messages around the clock. You may need to work a 12-16 hour shift and will have to allocate portions of the 24-hour day to personal or sleep breaks coordinated with the schedules of others on your virtual team.

Virtual meetings differ from face-to-face meetings, and there is a specific skill set that you will need to be successful. Daniel Cochece Davis and Nancy Scaffidi (2007) assert that every member of a virtual team needs to be self-motivated. Although employers are optimistic about personal self-motivation as they appoint employees to virtual teams, team members may not always work efficiently due to cultural backgrounds, methods of communication, and individual perceptions on the best way to contribute to the teams' progress. Some cultures work on an assignment until the work is completed, ignoring other demands until the current task is resolved. Other cultures treat time differently. Become familiar with everyone's working style and expectations. Discuss differences and arrange a schedule that accommodates all members. E-mail is generally preferred for communication, but that will not always be the most effective method for every individual on the team.

There may be many different cultures within a virtual team, and culture can influence how an individual functions within the team. "In virtual teams, specifically global virtual teams, members can reside in any country, speak a variety of languages, can be any age, ethnicity, or religion" (Davis and Scaffidi, 2007, p. 14). Colleagues may be communicating with you in their second, third, or fourth language. Therefore, it is imperative to pay close attention to their use of English. Most foreign educational institutions teach British English. This form of English uses a different spelling for some words in addition to differences in syntax and jargon. When a diverse virtual team generates a team document, it needs to be edited for a consistent style. The same statement applies to your own work when you generate material with colleagues in Spanish, French, or another language. Language is fluid, and unless you constantly update the nuances of a word's meaning it is quite possible to make a mistake in communicating a thought accurately. Working in a virtual team simply requires accuracy, understanding, and patience.

A good manager is knowledgeable about potential communication barriers prior to establishing a virtual team. Inform every team member regarding potential communication issues so everyone can recognize possible skill and cultural differences and smoothly pull their ideas and information together for a final report. This does not imply that team members can't solve communication issues as a project moves forward. They can, but some deadlines are easier to meet when a manager makes everyone aware of member differences initially. This saves time, avoids potential frustration within the team, and leads to a better result.

Another wonderful feature of the virtual world is that you can fully participate in critical team meetings from home during an emergency or illness. You can access every secure file and program in your office computer off-site thanks to software. An employee can present information and participate in critical meetings even when he or she can't be at their desk. SaaS companies are providing employers with new options for instant global communication and the restructuring of the workforce for greater efficiency and profitability.

FINAL THOUGHTS

Teamwork and the numerous meetings that populate professional life are expansions of interpersonal communication. Teams bring numerous colleagues together to solve a problem whether in the traditional face-to-face context or the virtual world. You need to work comfortably in both team formats. The traditional face-to-face meetings and teams continue in community organizations, educational institutions, religious organizations, nonprofit organizations, political organizations, and business. Virtual meetings and teams continue to evolve in corporations who have the financial resources and need for instantaneous solutions to planning issues. Each individual within a team possesses a specific expertise, personality, communication style, and work ethic. Everyone works together to achieve the employer's goals. Cooperation and understanding are necessary components for a productive team experience.

Teams challenge every aspect of your communication skills and style because each group situation has unique components and requirements. Good communication is the essential skill. Once your oral and written skills have evolved and been tested by colleagues and employers in countless situations, the topic of the next chapter becomes your next communication challenge: leadership.

KEY TERMS

Activists

Alienated followers

Bystanders

Conformists

Diehards

Exemplary followers

Followers

Groups

Isolates

Minutes

Participants

Passive followers

Pragmatists

Social elements

Task elements

Teams

Virtual meetings

Virtual teams

EXERCISES

1. Evaluate the other members of your blog group for their professionalism or lack of it.

2. Describe the type of follower you are. Can you change?

3. What challenges do you see in your ability to work in a virtual meeting? Participate in one if your school has the technical facilities.

4. Analyze your multitasking skills.

Decision Making, Problem Solving, Leadership, and Management

GOALS

After reading this chapter you should be able to:

- ✓ Explain and use the four types of decision making
- ✓ Differentiate among the four problem-solving methods
- ✓ Explain the steps of the reflective-thinking process
- ✓ Compare and contrast leadership and management
- ✓ Describe the traditional functions of management
- ✓ Explain the characteristics of good leaders
- ✓ Analyze your own leadership strengths

Problem-solving skills are highly desired in the corporate world. Plus, they are rather easy to present to an employer using a behavioral interviewing communication style. Problem solvers use concrete examples to shape their accomplishments as proof of an excellent work history. For example, you coordinated a fundraiser for a community organization and collected over $50,000 for the first time in the group's history. In discussing the project, you articulate a brief background of the group, its existing problems, an analysis of organizational issues, the plan itself as well as your strategy to raise the money, a financial description of when and how the money raised was spent, and an overview of the end result for this organization. Your thorough answer demonstrates to a potential employer that you possess analytical skills and the ability to get a task completed. In other words, you produce results. Your working life should consist of a number of positive results, reminding your current or potential new employers of your value to a company.

It takes time to find the appropriate solution for an existing problem. You must constantly observe, listen, and think about the corporate environment around you. How can you help the business to work more efficiently? Whenever you can save the employer money and still meet productivity goals, your value to the company is enhanced. The time it requires to solve a problem is worth every second of research and effort because a company that performs efficiently usually survives financially against corporate competitors. Your skills not only keep a company in business; they also keep you employed.

TYPES OF DECISION MAKING

There are many ways to make decisions in the business world. The type of task, the organizational culture, and the characteristics of employees all play a part in determining the best decision-making method to use when tackling a potential problem.

Vote

A **vote** is when you tally how many people are for or against an idea. This is a simple form of decision making. Whichever side of an issue receives 51% of the vote is the winner. You might be asked if you are in favor of a certain policy or rule, which person you'd like to move into a position, or other similar types of basic decisions. Typically, when a vote is required, there is a lot of factual discussion and disclosure of the various sides of an issue before you take a vote. Companies also may use a vote as a last resort when a decision is required and employees cannot come to an agreement.

Leader Mandate

In the **leader mandate** type of decision making, a leader makes all of the decisions. A good leader gathers information and input from everyone who will be affected by the action and makes an informed and rational decision. Of course, if the leader is power hungry and arrogant, he or she makes decisions without the input of others. If followers are happy with a leader's decisions, and the leader's communication is effective, employees will probably be satisfied with the leader mandate. For example, the military thrives on this type of decision making. If the leader is inept and unreasonable, employees may be extremely dissatisfied if they don't have input into a decision that affects them. This situation usually leads to low morale within an organization.

Compromise

A compromise decision happens when people working as a team negotiate a solution. **Compromise** consists of each side giving up a little of what it originally wanted. As negotiations occur in any work environment, compromise is taking place—especially between workers and management. Think about negotiating contracts. Each side comes in with unrealistic expectations, and then they begin the compromise process. For example, management offers employees a low deductible on their health care plan if they accept a $1 million lifetime cap on coverage. One of the hazards of compromise is that no one is really happy with the decision negotiated.

Consensus

Consensus happens when all parties concerned discuss all sides of the problem and arrive at a solution. The critical importance of a true consensus decision is that everyone is willing to stand behind the decision. They may not all be happy with it, but they all agree that the solution generated is indeed the best one. Consensus is reached through interpersonal persuasion, enlightening everyone with new information or new ways to look at old information, and further exploration of the issue.

The type of decision making needed to solve a problem varies with the complexity of the issue, the time available for reaching a decision, and the employees asked to participate in the process. You will probably experience each of these decision-making techniques during the course of your working career.

PROBLEM-SOLVING MODELS

As with decision making, there are various methods for solving problems. The specifics of each situation will dictate which problem-solving model would be most likely to generate an effective solution.

Brainstorming

Groups typically use brainstorming to generate ideas. The key concept behind **brainstorming** is to generate as many ideas as possible in the shortest amount of time. You appoint one person to jot down everything expressed. People quickly say what comes to mind, and others use what they hear to stimulate their own creative thinking and express their thoughts. Participants shouldn't evaluate or comment on any of the ideas generated during a brainstorming session.

Brainstorming creates lists of goals, solutions to problems, options for using technology, ideas to improve morale, etc. After you have generated a list of ideas, evaluation begins. Everyone analyzes the potential of each idea to achieve the group's goal. The goal of many brainstorming sessions is to present the top three ideas to the supervisor with an explanation of why each of them can solve the problem. Brainstorming is a technique that can also be used as a component of any of the following models.

Nominal Group Technique

The **nominal group technique** is basically a ranking system. Group members individually rank a list of options, solutions, goals, etc. and then average the scores. For example, an outstanding employee of the year committee might use this model to make a decision. Let's say there are 10 nominations. The committee looks at the list of names and whittles it down to the top 4 based on criteria they generated for the nomination process. Next, they interview the nominees. Once the interviews are complete, rather than discuss the candidates to make the decision, the committee ranks the candidates numerically instead. Then you average the rankings to find the employee with the best score.

The advantages to this model are that each individual has a say in the decision, and there is no influence from a boss or supervisor, who may be a member of the team. The disadvantages of this model are that sometimes the best person doesn't win. For instance, look at the following totals.

Nominee 1:   1, 2, 1, 1, 1, 2, 1   =   1.285
Nominee 2:   2, 1, 2, 2, 2, 1, 2   =   1.7142
Nominee 3:   3, 3, 3, 3, 3, 4, 3   =   3.1428
Nominee 4:   4, 4, 4, 4, 4, 3, 4   =   3.8571

These totals make it very clear that Nominee 1 should win. However, consider the situation with the following scores.

Nominee 1:   1, 2, 3, 1, 1, 4, 4   =   2.2857
Nominee 2:   2, 3, 4, 3, 2, 1, 2   =   2.4285
Nominee 3:   4, 4, 1, 1, 3, 3, 1   =   2.4285
Nominee 4:   3, 1, 2, 4, 4, 2, 3   =   2.7142

Nominee 1 wins in both cases. In the first scenario, most members of the committee will be satisfied with the decision. Usually if our second choice ends up winning, we can live with it. In the second scenario, three of the committee members ranked the actual winner in the bottom half of the candidates. Notice how close the numbers are between Nominees 1, 2, and 3. Committee members can be very unhappy and angry when the numbers shake out like this. What you thought would be a fair, impartial method does not always produce a unified result.

Delphi Technique

Groups use the Delphi technique when they are not meeting face-to-face, when there are power players who try to manipulate others in the group, or when underlings would sense pressure to conform to powerful members in a group. Once the group discusses the problem or issue, the **Delphi technique** is implemented by having everyone write a reaction, an assessment, or fill out a questionnaire about the problem or issue. In some applications of this technique, respondents remain anonymous. They send their comments to a central person who synthesizes all the ideas and sends them back to the group for further review. This process can occur as many times as necessary until the group reaches a decision.

The Reflective-Thinking Process

The reflective-thinking process is derived from John Dewey's (1910) classic work, *How We Think*, in which he described five basic steps in scientific reasoning. The reflective-thinking process has been adapted into a variety of problem-solving models. Gerald Phillips developed The Standard Agenda—"the most complete, the most flexible, and a time-tested method for problem-solving discussion" (Young, Wood, Phillips, and Pedersen, 2007, p. 11). The Standard Agenda has six steps that take the group through the reflective-thinking process.

Reflective thinking is "systematic" and "orderly" thinking. You'll find that many professionals approach problem solving in this manner. While your teachers may have given you rubrics of their criteria for figuring out your grades, in the workplace, human resources will require you to submit a rubric for interviewing individuals. Long gone are the days where you could simply look at résumés and determine whom you want to hire. Now you need to progress through the reflective-thinking process and submit each step of decision making for approval before moving to the next step in the process.

The purpose of the **reflective-thinking process** is to keep communication on track while problem solving. There are a few key steps that must be followed to allow a group to arrive at an optimal solution. The group members must understand the procedure. They must also be flexible enough to work back and forth between the steps. The format that follows presents a reliable process for reaching a decision (Young et al., 2007).

Step 1: Understanding the charge.   Group members must understand the task. We have seen numerous groups, both at the student and professional level, begin problem solving before the members realize what it is they are supposed to accomplish.

Understanding the charge means being able to answer the following questions: What is the goal of the group? Who formed the group and why? What resources are available to the group (including financial, material, technological, and human support)? When must the group make its final report? What form must the report take? Who gets the report?

Step 2: Understanding and phrasing the question.   Once the group members understand their mission, it is time to define the problem. Often group members assume everyone understands the problem, but they may not. Some individuals come to group projects with varying opinions and thoughts based on past experiences with similar assignments, and thus fail to approach the problem as a new entity.

During this phase, the group must determine exactly what the issue is that requires a decision. To do this effectively, the members should establish a discussion question. You typically phrase discussion questions in the following manner: Who should do what about what? An effective discussion question could be:

Which candidate in the pool will be the most effective to help us progress with our company goals?

Step 3: Fact-Finding. During fact-finding, members should collect as much relevant information about the issue as possible and exchange the collected information with each other. To achieve these goals, interactions must focus on (1) critical examination of the facts by all members, (2) whether the facts should alter the phrasing of the original discussion question, and (3) whether you have gathered enough information to proceed.

To be effective problem solvers, members must collect all the necessary facts. It is often difficult to determine when this step is actually finished. For our discussion question, the group would determine what requirements are necessary for the candidate in terms of level of education, degree, job requirements, and so forth.

Step 4: Establishing criteria. By now members are usually ready to jump to a solution, but there is one additional step. **Criteria** are the standards by which we judge people and things. Everyone uses criteria; you have standards by which you judge restaurants, movies, music, and so forth. Instructors have standards by which they judge speeches, assignments, papers, and exams. Instructors cannot just put a "B" on a paper because it "feels" like an above-average paper. Instead, they need to know what they are looking for and how they'll know it when they see it. Criteria tell us how we know a good solution when we see it.

The standard form for criteria is "Any solution must . . ." You would substitute words for "solution" as necessary. If we were hiring an entry-level PR person for our company, we would say, "In order to be hired, a candidate must . . ." and the group would develop a specific list of requirements such as:

- Have an undergraduate degree in Public Relations
- Have experience writing news releases, designing flyers, and creating promotional and marketing campaigns
- Have a cover letter with no typographical errors
- Have a proven record of community service

Note the difficulty with one of these criteria—how do the committee members define "proven record"? The first three criteria are objective; the fourth is subjective and you need to define it more clearly in order to proceed.

Do not move past the criteria step until you have defined and prioritized all criteria. A concrete definition of items is important so you have objective, concrete statements with which to work. Prioritization of the criteria is important in case you have more than one candidate who meets the same number of criteria. If two candidates meet two of the criteria above (Candidate A has the degree and experience but no community service, while Candidate B has community service and experience but no degree), you need to be able to tell which candidate is the better choice. So you need to prioritize your criteria—in this case our company cannot hire anyone without an undergraduate degree, so that is ranked first. We also cannot hire anyone without experience, making that our second criterion. However, lack of community service or a possible typo is not a deal breaker in this particular company, so we rank them lower.

Step 5: Discovering and selecting solutions.   In this step, group members brainstorm a list of solutions and select the best one. Notice that we do not even mention the idea of solutions until this step. Groups must gather facts and establish criteria before they consider the solutions. After those steps have been completed, group members brainstorm solutions. Remember, participants should *generate*, not *evaluate* ideas while brainstorming. Suppose your group is solving a problem of low morale in the organization. You collect data and develop criteria for your solution (such as it can't cost over $200, or it needs to be able to be implemented immediately). Then you would brainstorm possible solutions—such as having an employee appreciation lunch, giving out movie tickets to the most productive employee on a weekly basis, or having a rotating parking place reserved for someone who performs extraordinary work.

In the example we are using, there is nothing to brainstorm. Each candidate is a potential "solution" to the problem: a job opening. But note that we have not been allowed to access any résumés until the work leading up to this step was completed.

Next, we systematically evaluate each of our solutions against each of our criteria. It is often useful to create a matrix.

Solutions	Candidate A	Candidate B	Candidate C	Candidate D
Degree in PR				
Experience				
No typos				
Community Service				

ETHICAL ENCOUNTERS

How ethical is it to list the community service you did that was required as part of your fraternity/ sorority membership under its own résumé heading instead of indicating that it was required?

You could simply indicate "yes" or "no" in each of the boxes, but what about variations of degree? Most HR departments now require problem solvers to specify a point system. So your evaluation could look like this:

BS degree in PR
   10 = yes
   0 = no

Experience in PR
   8 = ran a campaign for real-world clients
   6 = ran a campaign for class assignment
   4 = wrote several flyers, PSAs, newsletters, or press releases
        for a company
   2 = wrote flyers, PSAs, newsletters or press releases for a class

No typos in paperwork
   6 = none
   3 = 1 or 2
   0 = more than 2

Community service
   5 = performed self-initiated community service
   3 = performed community service while a member of a
        campus organization
   0 = none

At this point, the group needs to discuss whether or not, and to what degree, each candidate matches each criterion. Criterion #1 is simple—candidates either have a degree or they don't. But criterion #2 has some gray areas to consider. Maybe you can't tell from the résumé whether the work was for business clients or for a class. Maybe there are multiple campaigns versus just one. Maybe one committee member perceives one thing after reading the candidate's paperwork while another member perceives something else. You will need to discuss these perceptions and facts in order to reach some sort of agreement.

Once committee members score each candidate against the criteria, it should become evident which candidate is the best hire.

Step 6: Preparing and presenting the final report.   The last phase is reporting your findings. The report is prepared in the format requested by the person who formed the group. If submitting a written report, please refer to chapter 6. We discuss group presentations in chapter 9. In the case of the job hire, your final report is the recommendation to HR. They may or may not require an extensive report with all of your minutes of meetings, rankings of candidates, and other materials.

When Does Reflective Thinking Yield a Bad Solution?

Do not be lulled into a false sense of security. The Standard Agenda helps people make the best decisions possible through systematic thinking. However, there are times when a group doesn't use The Standard Agenda effectively. Potential pitfalls when using The Standard Agenda are:

- Members do not accurately assess the problem
- Members do not gather all the necessary facts
- Members do not accurately analyze the facts
- Members fail to construct a good set of criteria
- Members do not systematically apply the solutions to criteria

Problem solving is time consuming and yet rewarding if everyone in the group fully participates in reaching a productive decision. The key to resolving any issue is to be as logical as possible in how you evaluate facts/candidates. It is important to be as honest and fair as possible in discussing how you plan to reach your decision before you establish criteria; once the criteria are in place you must apply them to the process. Criteria should not be changed after-the-fact. This is unethical except in instances when the problem solving cannot be completed based on the current criteria. Once evaluation begins, a solution is not far behind.

LEADERSHIP AND MANAGEMENT

While there are numerous theories about leadership and management, scads of books on each topic, how-to lists and information galore, the foundation of any good leader's or manager's reputation rests with their excellent communication skills. "A supervisor's communication competence appears to have a greater influence on employee outcomes than a supervisor's leadership style" (Madlock, 2008, p. 71).

Organizations flounder when employees are unaware of what is happening as policies shift, personnel changes, new technology replaces current technology, departments merge, unqualified personnel are promoted over more competent employees, the local press reports fraud within corporate accounting, and no one in the company communicates these changes. Each aspect of a company's daily operations needs to be assessed by a manager/leader and then analyzed to determine which employees need to be informed about decisions. Open communication creates a sense of belonging and pride in a progressive organization.

The concepts reviewed below continue to evolve with the complexities of global corporate expansion, the influence of new technologies on interpersonal communication, and the influence of cultural differences on language and behaviors.

Management

Managers are the people in charge of getting things done. Management theories emerged at the turn of the nineteenth century, and were either discarded, revised, or updated as the workplace evolved. The first management theories were scientific. People like Frederick Taylor (the father of scientific management) believed there was only one way to do things and advocated a specific formula. Others like Max Weber shifted this thinking and advanced a bureaucratic theory of management. The corporate structure was a hierarchy, with workers reporting to people above them in the structure. In the mid-1950s theorists focused on the human element in managing people. Theorists next began examining contingencies and situations. They began to acknowledge that each individual is different, each situation is different, and those differences necessitate different management styles.

Today, corporate structure and communication change so rapidly that anyone who becomes a manager needs to possess some basic tools—and good communication skills head the list of basic tools.

The list below includes some of the major theorists who have impacted the field of business communication. Research their backgrounds and their theories about management. Share your findings with classmates and compare your impressions.

Frederick Taylor	Max Weber	Elton Mayo
Rensis Likert	Mary Parker Follet	Henry Fayol
Abraham Maslow	Douglas McGregor	Robert Blake and Jane Mouton
Joan Woodward	Peter Drucker	Peter Senge

Overview of Management Duties Today

Managers have a number of duties. They are responsible for seeing projects through to completion with the least amount of cost and in the least amount of time. They need to manage the use of company resources—both equipment and personnel—efficiently and effectively. Meeting the goals of the company requires managers to plan, staff, organize, lead, and regulate. Planning includes deciding the best course of action for a project, and being capable of handling the situation when something goes wrong. Staffing involves both hiring the right people and training them to do the work needed for the company. Organizing means deciding how to use people and time most efficiently to complete a project. Leading includes communicating what the company needs, motivating employees, and building teams. Regulating requires the ability to monitor productivity and results and to discipline when necessary. Do you see yourself enjoying these tasks?

Think about how communication skills impact each of these tasks. How do you handle a crisis, build teams, control productivity and people, discipline, or train without good interpersonal skills? If you choose to move into a management position, you need to make sure that all of your communication skills are excellent. Many managers never thought they would be in the position of running a department, division, or company when their careers began. They were given the opportunity to serve in a responsible position by superiors who carefully observed their skills while working with the organization—and they liked what they saw.

Although you may feel invisible within an organization as an entry-level employee, you are not. Your attitude about work and the people around you is constantly visible. It is very important to perform professionally in every job you hold throughout your life. As a new employee or an established employee: your written work needs to be concise and clear; your verbal responses to colleagues and clients need to be thoughtful and articulate; your behavior needs to be appropriate; you need to be a problem solver and find ways to make things work; and you need to remain optimistic in your attitude regarding change and the future. An employee with this professional manner stands out in any organization and superiors are likely to move someone with these communication skills into a management track within the company. If you want superiors to consider you for a management position, there is no timeline on how long the process can take. It is your responsibility to demonstrate professional skills and to project a professional image continuously.

LEADERSHIP

Just like management theories, leadership models also evolved over the years. There has been an explosion of leadership theories. It sometimes seems as though leadership is a marketing ploy or a commodity—as though leadership is something that can be acquired by reading the right book or attending a seminar. While studying all aspects of leadership will help you target areas in which to improve your skills, there is no single step to becoming an effective leader.

Leadership ability is judged over a period of time. Your interactions and behavior on the job will determine whether you are perceived as a leader. Some basic leadership theories will help you develop leadership skills.

Difference between Management and Leadership

The basic difference between a manager and a leader is that managers make sure the work gets done while **leaders** inspire others in addition to accomplishing the task. Think about the numerous tasks a manager must accomplish each day: making sure people are at work and doing their jobs, performance evaluations, running meetings, establishing and maintaining schedules, and so on. They have to make sure that all of the jobs are executed properly so the company runs smoothly and makes a profit. Leadership is a little more nebulous. It involves inspiring people in addition to running a solid working environment. A manager can assist you with your work, but a leader instills in you a desire to do your work and do it well.

Can you be a good manager and not be a good leader? Absolutely. For example, Seth makes sure everyone is doing their job, processes all the paperwork, keeps the office organized, and meets deadlines. His division completes every assignment on time; employees get their jobs done. He talks to employees when something needs to be communicated. However, there is no vision of being better. No feeling of belonging to the company. No shared goals or dreams. No one is particularly inspired to work longer hours or accomplish tasks differently.

Can you be a good leader and not be a good manager? Absolutely. For example, LaQuisha is perceived as a visionary. She consistently communicates what is going well and what needs to be improved to her employees. She shares this in a way that inspires them to work harder and to take pride in what they do. When she talks, employees listen. When employees talk to her, she gives them 100% of her attention. The morale in the division is high, and LaQuisha inspires everyone to do their jobs well. Her employees wake up each morning excited to go to work, and they take great pride in being a part of her division of the company. However, LaQuisha cannot keep up with her daily paperwork. Reports are often received late. Employees get to a meeting room, and the arrangements are incomplete. The supplies and equipment necessary to conduct the meeting are missing.

In either scenario, workers may step in and cover the shortcomings of their bosses. However, it is far more likely that employees will step in and cover for LaQuisha's missing managerial skills (slipping her a reminder before the meeting about what needs to be done, reminding her of deadlines, etc.) because she inspires people to do more to make the company successful and to share in the success as a team member.

If you can develop managerial and leadership skills, you will be a valuable asset to the company. Very few business professionals have developed both of these skills extremely well. Management skills are easier to demonstrate than leadership skills because the perception of colleagues is a dominant component of the leadership. You may perceive yourself as a leader, but the reality is that the perceptions of others will be more important in determining whether you are assigned a leadership position.

We like the visual representation of management skills depicted in this graphic by F. John Reh (n.d.).

As you can see, leadership comes after you master a number of other communication skills.

BRIEF OVERVIEW OF LEADERSHIP THEORIES

One leadership theory, the **trait approach**, can be summarized in one phrase: leaders are born not made. The theory asserted that certain personality types will be leaders, others won't. Leadership characteristics cannot be learned. Good leaders are decisive, intelligent, and responsible; they take initiative and have excellent communication skills. The trait approach dealt exclusively with traits of the leader and did not consider the needs of followers.

Other theorists realized that there wasn't a "one model fits all" explanation of leadership. They suggested there were styles of leadership: authoritarian, democratic, and laissez-faire. **Authoritarian** leaders make decisions and make sure the group follows them. Today you might find the authoritarian leadership theory labeled as "directive leadership style."

Democratic leadership is quite different from authoritarian leadership. A democratic leader solicits information from followers, taking people's needs into consideration when making decisions. Today you might find democratic leadership labeled as "consultative leadership style" or "participative leadership style."

Laissez-faire leadership is a "hands off" style. In this model, a leader allows followers to govern themselves with very little input or direction. Today you might find laissez-faire leadership labeled as "delegative leadership style."

As leadership theories evolved, theorists began to see the value in understanding the needs of the employees/followers that leaders were trying to inspire. Situational theories soon emerged where leaders were expected to take into account motivational theories that might inspire their followers to perform better. They were also expected to use different styles based on the situation before them.

In other words, the best leader for most discussion/task groups is going to be the one who is flexible. There are times when the leader needs to simply observe while colleagues run with an idea. At other times, colleagues may be unmotivated, and the leader should move into authoritarian mode, directing people. A democratic approach works well most of the time in discussion/task groups because the leader is constantly soliciting ideas and synthesizing feedback. However, if your colleagues reach an impasse during a discussion, you may need to become authoritarian and tell everyone what they need to do so time isn't wasted. As a leader, you will need to finesse your skills so you can communicate appropriately to those around you. It is important to move out of your normal comfort zone when dealing with others, especially if you usually rely on only one of these styles. As a leader, you need to be fair to everyone and use the appropriate leadership style at the right time. If you communicate caring about the success and well-being of others, you are more likely to lead an effective team.

Transactional Leadership and Transformational Leadership

James MacGregor Burns (1978) introduced a new perspective on leadership. He compared traditional leadership, which he called transactional, with a more complex style that he called transformational (Hackman and Johnson, 2009). **Transactional leadership**, as implied by its label, involves exchanging rewards for desirable outcomes. The leader tells you what needs to be done and rewards you for doing it. Transactional leadership essentially maintains the status quo. Good performance is rewarded; poor performance is corrected. Burns believed that **transformational leadership** was both empowering and inspirational, creating more than a mere exchange.

Many researchers have studied leaders to identify common characteristics. "The characteristics of transformational leaders identified by all of these researchers are strikingly similar. Five primary characteristics appear, in one form or another, in all of the classification systems dealing with extraordinary leaders" (Hackman and Johnson, 2009, p. 105). The five characteristics are:

- creative

- interactive

- visionary

- empowering

- passionate

Since transformational leadership can convert followers into leaders, these characteristics permeate transformed groups and organizations.

While exploring the concepts of leadership, you may encounter additional terms. All of the theories developed attempt to explain why some people are successful in motivating others to accomplish a task. We feel strongly that exemplary communication skills are integral to any leadership style.

- Max Weber wrote about charisma and leaders in the early twentieth century (Hackman and Johnson, 2009, p. 124). **Charismatic leadership** occurs when a leader has extraordinary talents, a radical vision for solving a crisis, and followers who perceive the leader's capabilities.

- Some transformational leaders can communicate a vision to followers—a concise description of the direction in which a group or organization is headed. The vision attracts commitment and energizes people; it creates meaning for followers; it establishes a standard of excellence; and it bridges the present and future (Hackman and Johnson, 2009, pp. 114–115).

- **Servant leadership** is a new buzzword in leadership theory. A servant leader uses the same techniques outlined in transformational leadership; but what makes this style different is that the leader feels his or her goal is to serve the followers.

• **Facilitative leadership** involves gathering information from the team to create shared knowledge. However, when you ask for input, you should let your group know what you will do with it: Will you do what they determine is right as a group? Take the information under advisement and tell them what will happen? Being honest and up-front is important.

Characteristics of Good Leaders

Kristina Ricketts (2009) identifies the following as some of the characteristics of good leaders.

- efficient coaching skills
- confidence
- consistency between word and action—walk the talk
- creativity
- empathic listening skills
- visionary tendencies
- ability to inspire
- long-term focus
- ability to balance individual needs and team needs
- awareness of realistic conditions
- strong self-esteem
- sense of priorities
- service mentality
- sincerity
- technical or contextual expertise
- trust
- willingness to share responsibility
- willingness to share credit or recognition

How many of these characteristics do you possess? Since self-assessment is central to leadership development, you may want to look on the Internet for self-assessment exercises related to leadership concepts. For example, motivation to lead (www.mindtools.com); locus of control, power profile, goal setting, and emotional IQ (www.queendom.com); type A/B personality (testyourselfpsychtests.com) to name just a few. Many of these sites offer a free "snapshot" report with no obligation to purchase the full results.

Peter Drucker, one of the most highly regarded experts on management principles, details the following traits for the ideal leader (Krames, 2008, p. 135).

- Possesses character and courage
- Creates a clear mission
- Instills loyalty
- Focuses on strength
- Does not fear strong subordinates
- Is consistent
- Develops tomorrow's leaders

Again, how do you measure up on this list of traits? What kind of activities or behaviors could you practice to enhance your skills? Can all of these skills be cultivated? At what age? Or is there a limit? An individual can improve certain skills, which enhances confidence for a business career, but can a totally introverted individual who lacks self-confidence transform into a leader? There is no clear answer to the question, and opinions vary dramatically. However, if you feel you are missing some of the skills necessary for leadership, you can certainly work to improve any area of weakness. Identify the skills which need improvement, and then read about and develop strategies that will make them stronger. Personal commitment and constant practice will help you perfect your skills.

What Sets a Good Leader Apart from the Rest?

Have you experienced examples of poor leadership in the following areas: teaching, coaching, supervising, etc.? Let's look at some of the qualities that separate mediocre leaders from the truly inspirational ones.

Good leaders recognize the contributions of employees. The recognition heightens commitment to group goals and maintains motivation to contribute. Employee contributions deserve acknowledgement, and exceptional contributions merit special praise. Leaders can set an example for mutual supportiveness by being generous with words that call attention to the good work of individuals. Sincere recognition that is distributed among employees strengthens the sense of pride in the organization; it also enhances self-respect and respect for the contributions of others (Young et al., 2007).

Excellent leaders are people who are not afraid to hire smart, articulate employees. Some individuals in corporate America are extremely threatened by people who might outperform them. Often they will choose a lesser qualified person to fill an opening or promotion. We agree with Peter Drucker, who believed that good leaders don't fear subordinates. For example, in our own department we were recently fortunate enough to hire a candidate who knows far more about communicating through modern technology channels than we do. She is an expert blogger and does research in interpersonal communication via various technology channels. We could feel threatened by her knowledge, but we don't. We are thrilled to have someone with those skills and knowledge join our department. People who hire a lesser qualified candidate because they are insecure or feel threatened and need to appear smarter are actually quite foolish.

Genuine caring about employees and the company is another essential quality for leaders to possess. You'll know instantly when you walk into companies that have caring leaders. For example, they may take time to influence the environment—providing a clean and safe working space; furnishing new technology and supplies to help employees be productive; supplying extras that communicate caring to employees. Rodale Press, for example, keeps a stock of organic granola bars and snacks in the break room for its employees and provides a yoga space for them to de-stress. These types of perks may seem unrelated to the work of the organization, but they send a message to employees that they are integral, important members of the enterprise.

Leaders can also promote a caring image by managing communication effectively: keeping employees informed about company policies and explaining the nuances, acknowledging achievement via a personal note or formal announcement, responding to questions and criticisms immediately and with a professional and receptive tone. Many of these items may seem "little," but attention to detail keeps employees informed and comfortable with a leader. So often, when change is taking place, employees are kept in the dark. But something as little as a note that says, "We don't have any new information this week, but we'll update you as soon as possible" keeps employees in the loop. Timely communication makes employees feel like the leader cares about them. It also keeps rumors at bay and lessens the chances that employees will become suspicious. A leader's nonverbal communication should also promote caring, whether it is eye contact when communicating or the fact that they are the first people in the office in the morning and the last to leave at night.

Sadly, it is much easier to identify a bad leader than a good one. The early years of your working life should be spent observing the actions of others as well as listening to what is said and then analyzing the follow-through of everyone around you. Your observation skills can assist you tremendously in figuring out how communication works or doesn't work in various situations. Experience makes you a better employee and a potential leader because you've analyzed the successes and mistakes of others to develop your own professional persona. If you have the opportunity to work with a remarkable leader, consider yourself fortunate, and let the person know you value the experience. It takes a lot of work and some special personal characteristics to be truly effective as a role model and motivational as a leader.

FINAL THOUGHTS

One of the biggest decisions you make leaving school is finding a job to become financially independent. Your passion for employment allows you to apply the training and skills you've acquired in a real-world setting. The more you work, the greater the opportunity to expand your skills—as long as you listen attentively, observe those around you, and evaluate your own performance in the workplace. Confidence in your abilities improves as you demonstrate your value to others. Each oral, written, and nonverbal message you send will communicate your decision-making skills.

Problem solving is another professional skill that is easy to demonstrate to colleagues. Rather than allow yourself to believe that the status quo is acceptable, it is useful to use your positive communication style to bring new ideas and ways of working into a company. If you can streamline a procedure, work effectively with difficult people, or recommend a new idea that makes money for the company, everyone will recognize your talent as a problem solver. In addition to articulating suggestions for change, your original ideas need to be presented in writing. A written analysis of a problem with your creative solution gives people time to consider your idea(s). The written document contains your name as its creator, which also reinforces your value to the organization.

The principles of management and theories of leadership are futuristic concepts as you start a career. It will take you a while to be promoted into a position of responsibility so you can demonstrate to everyone that you possess these skills. Until that happens, you have the opportunity each day to exhibit a positive attitude, a strong work ethic, excellent communication skills, terrific interpersonal skills, knowledge about new technologies, an ethical approach in all your behavior, and an optimistic outlook about the future. After all, aren't these the qualities of good managers and leaders? It is easier to become a manager/leader if you exhibit to others that you already possess these skills as a novice in the organization. Project professionalism from the moment you begin a career, and your career path should be satisfactory and rewarding.

KEY TERMS

Authoritarian leadership
Brainstorming
Charismatic leadership
Compromise
Consensus
Criteria
Delphi technique
Democratic leadership
Facilitative leadership
Laissez-faire leadership

Leader mandate
Leaders
Managers
Nominal group technique
Reflective-thinking process
Servant leadership
Trait approach
Transactional leadership
Transformational leadership
Vote

EXERCISES

1. Describe/analyze the leadership style of a manager at your school.

2. Describe the management style of someone in the workplace whom you admire.

3. Analyze an experience where you completed a project with consensus. How did you feel about the final decision?

4. Describe which problem-solving method you use a majority of the time.

5. How do you react to being told what to do by an authority figure? Why?

Presentational Speaking

There is a good chance that you will be asked to make a presentation at some point during your career. Although you may have wondered why an oral communication course was necessary in your academic studies, you will use those skills often throughout your professional life. Whenever you make a presentation, it is important to remember that your goal is to reach a target audience. For example, when speaking with business colleagues, you do not generally need to define your terms since the audience should be familiar with any specialized terminology. An audience of laypeople outside your organization would have a different set of expectations; so, first and foremost, know your audience, whether subordinates, upper management, the board of trustees, or the general public. Business colleagues will pay close attention to the structure of a presentation. Time is valuable, so your ability to cover the topic efficiently, use technology effectively to enhance the presentation, and present the necessary information logically, concisely, and memorably will be important. Each presentation is an opportunity to demonstrate that you are an asset to the organization.

Colleagues want to work with a professional rather than with a person who makes obvious mistakes in speaking and writing. Such mistakes are easy to document and remember during performance evaluations and can restrict your career potential in an organization. If your goal at the outset of your career is to become a manager or run your own business, then you need to project a competent, polished image to colleagues daily.

Colleagues and staff see and hear your presentational style every day as you interact with them. Although some individuals consider the time spent with colleagues and clients as "social" conversation, every conversation contributes to how others perceive you. The personal qualities you project as you speak give others the opportunity to envision a future for you at a higher level in the company. For example, whenever you are given time to speak to your boss or supervisor, it is critical to be clear and concise in delivering your idea(s) while paying close attention to the time you were given for the meeting. If your boss gives you one minute, make sure you can state your idea(s) in 60 seconds or less. Supervisors are quite busy, and they appreciate employees who do not waste their time. Therefore, organize your thoughts before talking to a superior.

As you advance in responsibility, you may have to present specific ideas and reports to one person (your boss), a few people (colleagues), or a group (a corporate division). The general purpose of a presentation is usually to inform or to persuade. There are some presentations that combine these two purposes. It is useful to select the appropriate strategy for your remarks to make them easily understood by the listener(s).

In order to design an effective presentation in the workplace, you need to do the following:

1. Choose your general purpose: informative or persuasive
2. Confirm your topic
3. Prepare your key, goal, and thesis
4. Research, organize, and outline
5. Practice and delivery

CHOOSE YOUR PURPOSE

While this is probably going to be obvious if you've been asked to speak, it is important for a speaker to fully consider the purpose of the presentation: is it informative or persuasive? For example, you may be explaining the new online payroll system to the rest of your colleagues. The purpose of the presentation would be **informative speaking** because you are simply providing information to everyone. **Persuasive speaking** occurs when your purpose (goal) is to get the audience to change an attitude, belief, value, or behavior. What if you need to submit a reorganization plan to the boss for making the division work more effectively? You have to persuade her that your plan is best for your division. Or you may need to persuade colleagues to stop doing personal business on company time. If you are asked to convey information about a new policy, it may be more complicated to determine your purpose. Are you simply giving information about the policy, or are you expected to persuade employees to embrace it? Or is it a mixture of both? Knowing your purpose will help you to shape your comments in the most dynamic, effective way.

CONFIRM YOUR TOPIC

Most often, when someone asks you to speak, they give you the topic. The supervisor may ask you to present an update on a project at the weekly meeting, or to teach a group about a new program. Basically, these are informative presentations. If you are a manager, you may be the impetus for the presentation. In this case there may be corporate news to share with colleagues. No matter what the topic is, there are a couple of things you need to consider as you analyze it—(1) is the topic specific enough to present all of the information? and (2) will the information you select fit into the time constraints?

Time is of the utmost importance to your listeners. Colleagues have numerous work-related duties and usually have a packed daily routine. Americans live in a monochronic culture where everything runs by the clock. People are extremely fussy about deadlines and time limits. Professionals get intensely annoyed when someone abuses their time, which could have been spent addressing other demands. Make sure to narrow your topic enough to deliver all of the information within the time limit.

PREPARE YOUR KEY, GOAL, AND THESIS

Decide on the organizing key to your speech. Prepare the goal statement and thesis for informative speaking. If you took a basic oral communication or public speaking class, these elements should sound familiar. As you design your presentation, these elements will help you focus so that your information possesses continuity.

Key

The **key** is a word that describes the similarity among your three main points. Examples of a key are: steps, aspects, characteristics, parts, areas, or reasons. One of our colleagues, Bia Bernum, alerted us to the fact that her students grasped the concept of a coherent presentation when she used the term "key" to describe how the three main points fit together. If you don't have three related areas, your speech is likely to wander and end up as "everything you ever wanted to know about x," or it will be so disjointed that people won't understand what you are talking about. An exception to the rule would be if you are giving a "highlights" speech—for instance at the beginning of an academic year, a president might begin the semester with a "For your information" presentation where she lists a number of pieces of information that are unrelated to one another, but everyone needs to know about them. For a polished informative presentation, however, you need a key. Once you know whether you are speaking about *steps* in a process, or *characteristics* of an environment, or *events* in a campaign, or *aspects* of a problem, it is easier to connect the main points. For example, let's say your human resources department just determined that there is not enough accountability in the question-asking process of interviewing. They have decided to add three new steps to the hiring procedure. Your key is "steps," and each of your main points will explain one of those steps.

Goal

The goal is what you want as an end result of the presentation. Remember that a presentation is about gaining a specific audience response. We like the following goal format for informative speaking:

> After my presentation, I want my employees/colleagues to understand that . . . (basic information).

In the human resources assignment example, the goal would be:

> After my presentation, I want my employees/colleagues to understand that there are three new steps in the hiring policy.

The **goal** includes the **general purpose** (an informative presentation) and the **specific purpose** (explaining the three steps). You are not persuading employees to embrace the policy; you are simply informing them of the new policy and how it works.

Preparing the goal for persuasive speaking. Persuasion deals with changing the attitudes, beliefs, values or actions of the receiver. As you plan your corporate persuasion, whether it is interpersonal or in a public speaking setting, it is important that your goal is clear in your own mind. Are you trying to convince (change an attitude, value, or belief), reinforce (strengthen an attitude, value, or belief) or actuate (change an action). We like the following formats:

> After my presentation, I want my employees/colleagues to believe that . . .

> After my presentation, I want my employees/colleagues to believe more strongly that . . .

> After my presentation, I want my employees/colleagues to . . .

Examples:

> After my presentation, I want my employees/colleagues to **believe that** our security team is top notch. (Audience currently doesn't believe this)

> After my presentation, I want my employees/colleagues to **believe more strongly that** management is doing its best in these tough economic times. (Audience currently believes this)

> After my presentation, I want my employees/colleagues **to recycle all paper products and aluminum cans.** (Audience currently is receptive to the idea—no need to convince—but needs to be motivated to change behavior).

Thesis

The **thesis** for the informative speech includes the main points in the presentation. This would read:

> After my presentation, I want my employees/colleagues to understand that the three new steps in the hiring policy are approval of phone interview questions, approval of on-site interview questions, and approval of conversational topics for meals.

Once you have your key, goals, and thesis for the informative speech you can begin to construct its outline.

RESEARCH, ORGANIZE, AND OUTLINE

By the time you are searching for a job, you should have had either high school or college classes that taught you how to gather research. We won't review that process here but urge you to use those skills to acquire the facts and information necessary to support your presentation. The most up-to-date information is important for credibility in the presentation. You also should have learned about organizing your material into an outline. You should be familiar with the basic organizing scheme of dividing your topic into major ideas with supporting material; that each statement under any main point should support that point. If you don't understand how to do this, it is time to get some outside instruction. We will spend some time talking about basic speech structures for outlining a presentation. Whether you have five minutes or eight hours to present, this is a tried and true structure for giving information.

The Informative Structure

Any informative speech consists of an introduction, body, and conclusion. Speakers often compose the body of the speech before writing the introduction and conclusion.

Introduction.   The introduction should include all of the following:

- *Attention-getting device*: Prepare the audience to listen. Quotations, striking statements, current events, visual aids, or illustrations give momentum to your speech.

- *Relate to audience*: Audiences won't listen if they don't understand why the information is relevant to them.

- *Credibility*: Establish why you are the one who should be talking about this topic. If you have a title, this step is not necessary ("Here is Trevor Stravinsky, the Vice President of Finance, to give us an update on the budget situation.") If you don't have a relevant title and are introduced to give a training session or to run a seminar, state your credentials.

- *Preview*: Share your topic with the audience (reveal your main points). A simple statement such as "Today's presentation will cover X, Y, and Z" will suffice, but a clever transitional statement helps stimulate audience listening.

Body.   There are usually three or four main points with supporting material in this section. It is customary to state the most important point of the body first. Be sure you have effective transitions between each of the points.

Conclusion.   The conclusion should include the following:

- *Review*: Remind the audience of the main points covered in the body of the speech.

- *Restate the relevance*: Reiterate why your information is important to your listeners.

- *Concluding statement*: Some business presentations require a formal concluding statement. On other occasions, simply thanking the audience for their attention may be sufficient.

This format should work for almost any informative presentation you would be called upon to give in a business setting. The next section reviews persuasive formats.

The Persuasive Structure

There are a few basic persuasive structures—statement of reasons, problem-solution, and Monroe's Motivated Sequence—that you can employ depending on the purpose of your presentation. We will review each briefly.

Statement of reasons.   In a statement-of-reasons structure, a speaker reveals the persuasive claim at the beginning of the speech and follows the claim with a number of reasons why the audience should accept it. Use this structure if you want to convince your audience to accept a claim. For example:

I want my employees to believe that it is in the company's best interest to freeze salary adjustments in order to:

- save jobs

- benefit all employees over the long term

- preserve current health-care benefits

Typically, the reasons are presented in order of strength. Each of the reasons needs to be fully documented with factual evidence. Each of these reasons would be a main point in the body of the speech.

Problem-solution.   A problem-solution structure is useful if you want to convince the audience someone should do something. In this structure, your main points are (1) the problem, (2) the solution, and (3) the advantages of the solution. For example, you are a manager at a company where employees are habitually late, and you want your administrator to believe that you require help to solve the problem.

I want my administrator to believe that employee lateness can be solved using a time clock system.

- Employee lateness is costing the company time and money.

- A time clock system would solve the lateness issue.

- Time clocks are inexpensive and will result in more employee productivity.

This structure is essentially a policy claim. You want someone else to do something about the problem, and you are working hard to convince the administrator or administrative board that there is indeed a problem with an easy solution available. Your emphasis in this speech is convincing them the problem exists, and they can help solve it. In the next speech structure, Monroe's Motivated Sequence, the emphasis is on motivating your audience to embrace a solution—you want the employees/audience to do something immediately.

Monroe's Motivated Sequence (MMS).   MMS is a five-part, action-oriented organizational pattern (German, Gronbeck, Ehninger, and Monroe, 2010). This organizational pattern is appropriate when the audience is not opposed to your topic; audience members just lack the motivation to perform an action. You'll see that there is a similarity between this structure and the problem-solution structure. However, this structure is more complex than the previous ones because you are attempting to get the audience to take action rather than simply agree with you. You need to ignore the statement-of-reasons structure to be successful with MMS. You are no longer stating a claim and giving reasons why someone should do something. With MMS you must describe a problem the audience faces, and then motivate them to action. The following is adapted from German et al., 2010:

I.   Attention Step

(Use an effective attention-getting device here)

II.   Need Statement

    A.   Make a definite, concise statement about the problem (avoid a circular argument).

    B.   Use one or more examples explaining and clarifying the problem. Be sure to include additional examples, statistical data, testimony, and other forms of support.

    C.   Show the extent and seriousness of the problem.

    D.   Make it clear that the problem affects the audience.

III.   Satisfy the Need

    A.   State the action you want the audience to begin (or stop).

    B.   Explain your proposal thoroughly.

    C.   Demonstrate with reasoning how your proposed solution meets the need.

    D.   Refer to practical experience by supplying examples to prove the proposal has worked effectively where it has been tried.

    E.   Forestall opposition by anticipating and answering any objections that might be raised against this proposal.

IV.   Visualize (use only 1 of the following)

    A.   Describe conditions as they will be in the future if the solution you propose is carried out.

    B.   Describe conditions as they will be in the future if your proposal is not carried out.

    C.   Use both the negative and positive potential results.

V. Request Action

(Tell the audience every detail they need to know in order to perform the action.)

So let's look at an example of a presentation using the MMS structure. For this example, the speaker is a manager whose goal is to motivate employees to save energy and reduce costs by powering down their computers at night and turning off lights when they leave their offices.

Attention step. You first need to get your audience's attention. The attention step in MMS is similar to the attention-getter in the informative speech. After hearing this step, the audience should say, "I want to listen!"

Showing the need. In this step you must convince the audience there is a problem that affects them. The first thing you do is state the problem; be clear and specific. To prove to your audience that this is indeed a problem, you will need to include lots of evidence in the form of supporting material. It is not enough just to say a problem exists—you must prove it. Obviously some problems require more evidence than others. If you want to prove your audience is stressed, it might not take much convincing. However, if you want them to believe that energy is being wasted, you may need a lot more factual evidence and emotional appeal to accomplish your goal.

Be careful not to reveal your topic in this step. The idea is to convince your audience that they face an urgent problem (company costs are eating into profits). You will show them what to do about it in the next step (save energy). Note the problem is company costs. If you say the problem is that the employees don't power down computers, you are building a circular argument.

Don't forget to link the problem with your audience; they must believe immediately it is indeed their problem. Think about the commercials for starving children in the developing world. You know the problem exists, but how many of you send money to help? If you don't, chances are the reason you don't send money is that you don't feel connected to the problem. It is something that happens "over there" and doesn't affect you personally other than the fleeting emotion you may feel when you see the commercial. The commercial does not resonate sufficiently for you to take action.

So in this step, you would present the audience with data on the monthly cost of utility bills and how that cost affects their raises and company profits. They have to believe that this issue directly connects to them. If they think that the money is coming out of the CEO's pocket, they may not care as much.

Satisfying the need.   You reveal your claim and tell the audience what it is you want them to do. There are five parts to this step. You must first reveal the action you want them to perform in a clear and concise manner (power down computers at night and turn off lights as they leave the building). Second, you explain what it is you want them to do. In some speeches, you will need a lot of explanation. In others, you will not. For this speech, the explanation is simple.

The third part is to explain how the action you want them to take solves the problem you outlined in the need step. You must use strong reasoning and factual support. You will have to provide calculations that show the overall savings their actions will have for their company.

The fourth part contains evidence that the solution has actually worked. You might use personal testimony, research studies, and citations by expert authorities to prove this point. What other companies have done this with success?

Finally, you design the fifth part to meet anticipated objections. Keep in mind you can't persuade people if they are arguing with your claim in their minds. In this part of the satisfaction step you need to refute any potential arguments the audience could be composing mentally. Here is where a thorough audience analysis comes in handy. You need to know *why* they aren't currently doing the action. They just don't think about it? Believe that it takes more energy to turn the computers and lights on and off than to leave them on? Each of these reasons necessitates a different angle. By the time you complete the satisfaction step, your audience should realize that executing your claim will solve the problem and that there are no obstacles to prevent them from doing so.

Visualization.   In this step, you want to show the audience how their world will be a better place if they perform the action you suggest. You can do this by describing how things will improve if they do the action, how things will worsen if they don't perform the action, or you can include elements of each. Show them the direct benefit they will enjoy by cooperating with the plan.

Requesting action.   In this step, you motivate the audience to begin the action. You need to give them every detail they need in order to do so. You might give them a handout that prescribes the specific actions they should take. Or you can give audience members a post-it with the necessary information in an easy-to-read list and encourage them to post it on their computer as a simple reminder. This section must end with a strong concluding statement.

Selecting a Structure for Miscellaneous Presentations

There are multiple situations where it may not be immediately clear whether you should use informative or persuasive structures. In these situations, always think about your purpose as you develop your remarks. Let's look at the following examples.

Business pitch.   A business pitch might be informative, or you might use any of the three basic persuasive organizational strategies adapted for your purpose. For example, let's say you have to pitch an idea to the boss. Some textbooks have "pitch outlines," but what is the purpose of your pitch? If it is to convince the boss that the company is losing money through employee theft, then you may want a statement-of-reasons structure. If it is to propose a solution to that problem, but the boss doesn't know about it, you may want a problem-solution structure. Use the MMS when the pitch is being made to an audience that already embraces or has little opposition to the idea, but just needs motivation to do it.

Crisis communication.   A crisis befalls your company. What speech structure do you use? It depends on your audience and your purpose. Are you communicating to the employees or the public? Is it strictly informational (there will be no bonus checks this quarter) or persuasive (convincing the public to maintain confidence in your company after an environmental disaster, corporate scandal, etc.)? Once you know your purpose for communicating, you can select the appropriate structure and craft it to fit the occasion.

Communicating good/bad news.   Are you simply informing audience members of a decision or event that impacts them in a positive or negative way, or do you need to go a step further and shape their reaction to the news?

Training speech.   Is there only the element of giving information to an audience or are you expected to persuade the audience to adopt the new software, incorporate a new procedure, and so forth? You may choose a mixture of the above structures.

Commemorative speech. You may have to give a commemorative speech for a retirement, a funeral, corporate anniversary, or other occasion. Here you will probably use a hybrid of an informative speech with elements of a persuasive speech to reinforce the fundamental theme of the presentation. The audience already knows the person or company. Hopefully they are happy for them (in the case of celebration) or sad to lose them (in the case of retirement or death). Decide on the most relevant points to highlight for the commemorative speech and then personalize your remarks. You need to present fascinating details about the person or company that connect and resonate with everyone in attendance. The creative use of language and examples in this type of speech will make it memorable for the audience. A commemorative speech is challenging and quite different from other presentations you make as a professional.

Always remember that you may need to finesse whatever structure you select based on the situation. For instance, if we want our boss to make a change because morale is low, chances are good he already knows that, so we don't have to delve heavily into the need step of the MMS. However, if we gave that presentation to the president of our company, she may need to be convinced that low morale is a problem, so we would include that step. Sometimes your audience already knows about the problem, in which case you modify your problem-solution structure to simply mention the problem, and then devote the bulk of your time on detailing a creative solution for the audience.

There are also numerous group presentations that rely on the presentational structures provided above.

Structure and Organization of Group Presentations

There are several types of **group presentations**, but we will mention four: symposium, roundtables, panels, and forums.

Symposium. The symposium refers to a presentation where a group is in front of an audience, and each person gives a portion of a prepared speech. There should be an introduction, a conclusion, and transitions between the speakers. The speeches should all last approximately the same amount of time, and each should flow seamlessly from the previous speaker, contributing to a perception of a unified whole. Everything that was discussed earlier on informative and persuasive speech structures apply to this type of presentation.

You need to think about the entire presentation with each participant presenting a main point or section. Therefore, in a group of five, for instance, one person might give the introduction, the next three people would each give information about a specific main point, and the fifth speaker would conclude the presentation. Dividing responsibilities in this manner makes it easy for the audience to listen and comprehend.

Roundtable.   The roundtable discussion consists of a moderator and group members having an actual discussion. The moderator can be a group member, or can be someone from outside the group. In a symposium, members prepare their remarks on a portion of a topic; in a roundtable, participants must be prepared to discuss the entire topic. A roundtable discussion is similar to a polite discussion among knowledgeable peers; there is generally no audience. This is a popular television format for journalists discussing topics of national interest (in this case, there is an audience, of course, but not in the studio. The audience is eavesdropping on the discussion). A roundtable discussion may be used for focus-group research where there is a set of prepared questions and a moderator who leads the discussion. Focus-group research is designed to obtain information from a group of people concerning their opinions or knowledge on a particular topic. They are commonly used for market research and for public opinion polls.

Panel.   A panel discussion is basically a roundtable discussion made up of expert panelists and held in front of an audience. Participants must enter the discussion fully informed about the topic. The group uses a moderator to keep the discussion moving, usually with pre-planned discussion points. The panelists hear the reaction of the audience as they speak. Some panel discussions allow questions from the audience near the conclusion of a presentation.

Forum.   Forum discussions directly involve the audience. Any talk show that you see usually has a forum component—the host asks the audience for input or questions. You can combine a forum with any of the group presentations mentioned above. For example you may find a presentation advertised as a symposium-forum, meaning there will be a prepared presentation given by multiple people followed by questions from the audience. Panel-forums do the same thing. Town hall meetings are one example of forums. Political campaigns use town hall meetings, as do numerous organizations and universities.

Tips for group presentations.   There are numerous tips that can make your presentation stand out. Every member should be in professional attire and dressed in similar colors. Dressing alike has definite psychological advantages because your group appears united. For example, notice how many political candidates use red, white, and blue in their attire. Be aware of your nonverbals during a group presentation. If every presenter is in front of the audience, it is essential that every member's attention be riveted on the speaker. As soon as members doodle, talk to one another, or fidget, they compromise the credibility of the entire group for an audience. If presenters can't pay attention to their own material, why should the audience?

Be sure to practice the presentation as much as possible. Many groups have each member design a portion of a presentation. However, if you don't rehearse the presentation as a team, you may make the mistake of more than one member communicating identical information without additional insights. The audience will notice the lack of organization. Without rehearsal, the verbal and physical transitions from one member to the next may not sound or look polished. One person may transition well to the next speaker, but another does not. Team members must look and sound as though they worked together. It is extremely difficult to work individually and make a presentation look like a coordinated project. A post-analysis critique is essential during this phase. If everyone just presents and then says "great job," no one really listened critically for the flaws in the others' presentations. Remember, just because you deliver information does not mean it is good.

It is useful to visit the actual space where the group will be presenting. Learn where the electrical outlets are, the technology available to you, and the best way to use the space; you want to avoid mistakes during the actual presentation. Sometimes team members find they have differing definitions of professional attire due to their division's dress requirements. Business colleagues accept these nonverbal differences in attire, but the general public may wonder why one presenter is wearing khakis and a sport shirt, while the others are in suits and ties.

Preparation is critical for every presentation you make. As you research a topic, question all of the facts you gather to make sure they are accurate. Make sure your research is exhaustive; don't rely on notes you made months or years earlier. If you overlook new research that contradicts the point you are making, your presentation will be compromised. The time you spend researching material and organizing it will help keep you focused and calm. Confidence in the material you put together, both written and visual, gives you the psychological edge you need to speak eloquently with colleagues, clients, and bosses alike.

PRACTICE AND DELIVERY

The effective delivery of a presentation is an obstacle for some speakers. It takes patience, practice, and confidence to translate written words and thoughts into a sincere personal vocal style. Your voice helps a prepared message resonate with listeners; excellent oral skills will make you stand out in business.

Practice

The old saying, "Practice makes perfect," is absolutely true. You should take the time to rehearse every presentation multiple times and with a clock. Articulating the words out loud will help you correct awkward phrasing. The more you rehearse, the greater the chance that the words in your speech will flow easily when facing your audience. No one will ever know how long it took you to prepare a good presentation—nor do they care. In fact, the most effective presentations often appear effortless. In addition to practicing pronunciations and phrasing, you need the presentation to fit the time limit you are given. Therefore, time each of your practice sessions. Your audience will appreciate the fact you finished within the time limit because they need to return to the daily demands of their schedule.

Remember, an audience of business professionals expects a polished presentation, so be prepared. There are no "do-overs" in the corporate world.

Delivery

There are three basic business delivery styles: impromptu, manuscript, and extemporaneous. The **impromptu** style (unprepared, "off the cuff") is used daily to communicate with colleagues. A great deal of daily discourse doesn't require the sequential development of an idea or a detailed response to a question. However, conversations with fellow employees or supervisors occasionally require more detailed explanation or an overview of a procedure. These situations test your ability to mentally organize a logical response using a standard verbal outline: introduction, body, and conclusion. These detailed impromptu answers can be challenging if you aren't prepared to share your expertise with others.

A **manuscript** style is self explanatory. A presentation is read from a prepared script. Although some disciplines and professional areas use this style, it is not an engaging performance style for the audience. Professionals know how to read and would prefer to listen to presenters highlight and explain key points. Audience members can take a copy of the presentation back to their offices to read or access it on their computers. Audiences prefer eye contact from a speaker and a chance to get a sense of their personality in a "live" or webinar situation; reading from a manuscript does not provide that immediacy. Politicians, news professionals, and corporate CEOs use a teleprompter to make the manuscript style work. In these presentations, audiences do not object to a read speech because a teleprompter creates the illusion that a speaker is looking at them during the presentation. The technology makes reading a presentation more acceptable.

The **extemporaneous** style is conversational speaking. It makes listeners feel as though they are important to you because you talk *to* them, not *at* them. Many presenters find this method of speaking slightly uncomfortable because they don't have a manuscript in front of them—only a few notes. The extemporaneous style requires the presenter to remain fully engaged with the topic and the delivery of the information to the audience throughout the performance. A topic outline or a few note cards becomes a guide for the entire speech. The speaker's mind and personality drive the material shared with listeners. An effective way to remain calm and vocally relaxed during extemporaneous performance is to imagine yourself holding a social conversation with the most influential, trusted person in your life—for example, morning conversation over breakfast with your grandmother at the kitchen table. If you can think of a person in your life with whom you were emotionally comfortable while talking, this mental image can be useful during your professional career in keeping your voice passionate and engaging.

A conversational speaking style is as natural and lively as you are when associating with family and friends. The important vocal qualities to use for stressing key words and ideas during a presentation are rate, projection, inflection. **Rate** refers not only to the speed or slowness of articulation skills but it also refers to the length of time the vowels within words can be used as an emphasizing tool while making a point. Stretching a vowel to make a point catches the listener's attention because the sound of the word is suddenly unusual. Southern speech in the United States uses vowel blends within words, which most audiences find pleasing and charming.

Projection is the physical energy behind your voice—sometimes so that you will be heard at the back of the room and sometimes to make a point. Fortunately, your voice is amplified through a microphone in the majority of business presentations, which eliminates the necessity of over projecting your voice and sounding forced. The only time projection skill is necessary is when an amplification system fails. It does happen. If you know how to project, you will be able to continue with your presentation without waiting for a technician to repair a microphone or sound system. Transitioning smoothly after a failure in technology keeps the presentation moving and demonstrates clearly to an audience that you have experience in public performance.

Inflection is the pitch range of your voice. It adds aural interest to a presentation because the higher and lower pitches of voice can emphasize words and phrases in a subtle way. Some presenters attempt to control their performance style so much that they sound monotonous and repetitive in everything they say. However, a conversational style gives you the opportunity to connect with an audience as a "real" person, even though the information you are delivering may be quite formal. Your voice is as unique as you are, so use its full potential to establish a professional identity.

If used well, visuals make portions of your presentation clearer and more memorable. Determine which concepts or portions of the presentation would benefit from visual reinforcement. Electronically generated visuals are the norm in business, with PowerPoint and streaming video clips as supporting elements. Ten percent of the total presentation time is normally the recommended limit for visual support. This time limit may be extended for special presentations such as a new product launch, however.

You should always rehearse all visual segments of a speech to make sure your oral transitions in and out of the visuals are as smooth as possible—as well as making sure you know how to use the technology itself. Nothing is worse than watching speakers attempt to use a piece of unfamiliar equipment, discovering too late that they do not know how to turn it on or how to load their information.

FINAL THOUGHTS

Presentational speaking is an excellent way to demonstrate your value to an employer. Whether you are presenting information by yourself or with a group of colleagues, the moment itself makes you visible in the company. A thorough understanding of the purpose for your presentation allows you to hone the research and structure necessary to achieve your goal of informing or persuading others with a professional demeanor. Selecting the proper content structure keeps you focused as you speak. The audience deserves an informed, poised, enthusiastic, and organized speaker.

Speaking in the professional world is somewhat relaxing because you know the material well through work experience and expertise. The audience is usually internal so everyone knows something about the topic and is eager to hear what you have to say. Since the audience is somewhat knowledgeable of the topic, your research must be accurate and up-to-date. The words you articulate to shape the presentation, your perceived personality, and the technology integrated into the presentation make your effort easy to evaluate. Preparation and practice are the key elements in giving a solid presentation.

New technology drives numerous business presentations (chapter 7). Therefore, your mental, physical, written, and verbal skills are tested throughout a presentation. In a web conference, you share your thoughts and research with others in "real" time. Members of a group can e-mail a question during your remarks, which you need to address aurally or send them visuals while you are speaking and interacting with them: a Power-Point, a graphic, or streaming video. You may also be typing e-mail responses to others as you speak. In other words, new technology requires adept multitasking skills to ensure that the correct visual material is forwarded immediately to colleagues who request it—while the speaker simultaneously remains focused on the topic. This scenario is the current cutting-edge style of presentational performance in business. New media allows a collaborative approach to presentations but requires attention to detail to weave technical support into the presentation.

KEY TERMS

Business pitch

Commemorative speech

Crisis communication

Extemporaneous

Forum

General Purpose

Goal

Group presentation

Impromptu

Inflection

Informative speaking

Key

Manuscript

Monroe's Motivated Sequence

Panel

Persuasive speaking

Problem-solution

Projection

Rate

Roundtable

Specific Purpose

Symposium

Thesis

Training speech

EXERCISES

1. Analyze things you do and don't enjoy while preparing and giving a presentation. Why?

2. Give a one-minute business pitch for a product.

3. Write a eulogy for yourself.

4. Give a commemorative speech (three to four minutes) for a high-school classmate.

5. Do a five-minute group presentation with your blog colleagues. Use some technology as part of the presentation.

Potentially Threatening or Uncomfortable Communication

CONFLICT IN THE WORKPLACE

We have stressed the importance of interpersonal excellence throughout this book. However, interpersonal communication doesn't always go

smoothly even when you are skilled in using language and nonverbal behavior. Conflict is inevitable in the workplace due to corporate policies, corporate culture, and the diversity of employees and managers.

Conflict occurs any time there is a disagreement between two or more people. Stephen Littlejohn and Kathy Domenici (2007) list six types of conflict:

- Data conflicts
- Interest conflicts
- Relationship conflicts
- Value conflicts
- Structural conflicts
- Moral conflicts

Data conflicts are caused by a lack of information, misinformation, different views on what is relevant, different interpretations of data, and different assessments of procedures. **Interest conflicts** are the result of perceived competition, or differences in procedural or psychological interests. **Relationship conflicts** are caused by strong emotions, misperceptions or stereotypes, poor communication, or repeated negative behavior. **Value conflicts** result from different criteria for evaluating ideas or different ways of life. **Structural conflicts** are caused by destructive interactions, unequal distribution of resources, unequal power, physical hindrances to cooperation, and time constraints. **Moral conflicts** result from differences of worldview or ideology (value differences are one aspect of moral conflict that tends to be more persistent and difficult to manage).

Disagreements can involve a policy, an approach to a problem, a scheduling issue, workload, use of technology, use of language, behavior, interpersonal differences, and so on. In a diverse working environment, employees see issues in totally different ways, including ways to resolve problems. While many people think conflict is undesirable, it is actually essential to any growing relationship. What is important is how you resolve conflict when it occurs.

Ineffective conflict resolution involves yelling and screaming, manipulating, issuing ultimatums, silence, walking out of the room, or refusing to discuss issues. While such behavior may seem unimaginable, it does occur in corporate America. These negative strategies leave participants feeling angry, used, scared, and/or frustrated.

Effective conflict resolution is comprised of spirited discussion, active inquiry, listening skills, critical thinking, and problem solving. The goal is to find a solution to the disagreement without creating animosity in a working relationship. If you are afraid of conflict, chances are that you have experienced ineffective conflict resolution in your lifetime. People who engage in effective conflict resolution tend to enjoy working through their differences to reach an acceptable resolution. A healthy working relationship between two people must involve an environment where participants can feel comfortable in resolving a disagreement. Each person wants to feel that his or her ideas have value and that there can be a mutual resolution—rather than one person winning and the other person feeling left out.

The potential for conflict exists everywhere in daily communication—from little things like how offices will be set up or who will make the coffee to larger issues like how to reduce expenditures to match the new operating budget. You can choose to escalate or deescalate most conflicts once you identify them. The decision is yours. When we use ineffective strategies, we escalate the conflict. For example, if you mouth off to a colleague or superior, you may escalate a conflict tenfold in addition to shortening your tenure with the company. What other choices do you have? Thinking carefully about how to respond to someone and choosing the right words and vocal tone are skills you can learn and use to deescalate a conflict immediately.

CONFLICT-RESOLUTION STYLES

In any interpersonal relationship, conflict is inevitable. Some people have a very negative connotation for the word "conflict." Conflict itself, however, is not bad. It simply means disagreement. However, if you handle the conflict or disagreement poorly, the result will be negative feelings for both individuals. Ralph Kilmann and Kenneth Thomas (1977) suggest there are five styles of handling conflict. The five styles vary in the amount of assertiveness and cooperation.

- **Competing** involves assertive and uncooperative behavior. People using this style pursue personal concerns at the expense of others. The style is power-oriented. When competing goes too far, it becomes **bullying**.

- **Accommodating** involves unassertive and cooperative behavior—the opposite of competing.

- **Avoiding** is both unassertive and uncooperative. It can involve **withdrawing** and **delaying**.

- **Compromising** involves moderately assertive and moderately cooperative behavior. It falls between competing and accommodating.

- **Collaborating** involves both assertive and cooperative behavior. People explore an issue to uncover underlying needs and work together to solve the problem.

The most effective communicators are able to apply each of the five styles as they relate to a specific situation. You should become familiar with each style and use the one that best enables you to handle a specific disagreement. Learn to assess the needs of both parties involved in a disagreement, so you can use the style most likely to result in both parties having a positive experience.

Competing Style

When it is important to "win" the conflict at all costs, the competing style is appropriate. This style is effective when you truly believe in something, or during a crisis situation where the conflict must be resolved immediately. For example, if two employees are fighting constantly and they cannot resolve personal differences, the supervisor may decide to transfer one person to another division. This style is, however, ineffective for most interpersonal relationships. Most people do not want to be dominated, and competitive responses close the door to further discussion. A competitor does not listen to others and is not concerned with their thoughts or needs.

We often get tired, however, of working with someone who always has to be right. Sometimes in the work environment, the competitive style can turn into the subcategory of bullying. Bullying occurs when a person must be right no matter what, and the person uses coercion, manipulation, or intimidation to propel you into doing something or believing something that is contrary to your normal instinct. This is an extremely difficult situation in the work environment. If someone tells you to "choose your battles," they might be indicating that you are unreasonably aggressive. Be sure you don't turn into an interpersonal bully who has to win every argument at any cost. Others will be uncomfortable working with you.

On the positive side, two people who enjoy a spirited discussion of an issue can also be using the competitive mode of resolution. Both individuals may be asserting themselves, wanting to win the discussion, and they have fun while trying to convince each other of the correctness of their position. This style is not comfortable for many people, but some people enjoy the vigorous banter and remain good colleagues after such a heated discussion.

Accommodating Style

When people subordinate their opinion to that of someone else to promote harmony in a relationship, they are using an accommodating style. This style develops when people are afraid of conflict, afraid to voice an opinion, or are so easygoing that they do not have a strong opinion one way or the other. However, if you have an opinion, you should not use this style. People who repress their own opinions in the workplace may become hostile or depressed. Sometimes they even play the martyr role with their language and behavior, which can be annoying to others.

You should articulate your opinions appropriately. For example, if Maureen asks Andrei what PowerPoint background he'd like for their presentation, and he says he doesn't care, he should not say, "Oh I hate that" when she picks one and designs the presentation. If he has only one dislike, he can say, "Anything is fine with me as long as it isn't pastel." If he has a list of things he dislikes, then he should not use the accommodating style. You should only use this style if you truly don't have an opinion and are willing to do what the other person wants to do without question or comment.

Avoiding Style

When people walk away from conflict, they are using an avoiding style. People using the avoidance style say, "I'm outta here," when a heated argument begins. They physically remove themselves from the situation. This style is important to use whenever there is any threat of physical or verbal abuse either to you or from you. When abuse is not an issue, the avoidance style is one of the least useful styles because nothing is resolved. One person leaves, but the problem remains.

There are two subsets of the avoidance style. Someone might **withdraw** from a conflict. This can occur for two reasons: (1) The person you are arguing with has no opinion on the topic or no needs that must be met. In this case, the person simply doesn't care to engage in the conflict. There is no reason to participate. (2) The person is truly afraid of conflict. The individual may have grown up in an abusive family and can't handle the emotional response brought on when people start raising their voices and arguing, even in good spirit.

Another subset of the avoidance style is **delaying**. Delaying happens when someone is too upset to continue with the conflict at that moment. Whenever you feel that you might say or do something that you'll later regret, it is wise to delay the conflict until you calm down and can express yourself appropriately. If you become emotional during conflict, this is a useful strategy so that you never fall apart in the office. Saying something like "I need to talk about this tomorrow" or "I'll come back in an hour to discuss it" lets the other person know that you aren't simply walking out. A break in the discussion is acceptable as long as you return to continue it and resolve the issue.

Compromising Style

When both people give in slightly to reach a solution, they are using a compromising style. In the same example with Maureen and Andrei and the PowerPoint background, Maureen wants a blue background, and Andrei wants a red tone. So, they decide to use the combination of red and blue for the background, and they choose purple. In this case, neither of them is getting what they really want, but they are both getting a little of what they want. A compromise can work well in situations where there is no other resolution, but in this example, both individuals would probably feel slightly cheated artistically.

Collaborating Style

When people work through the problem-solving process to reach the best solution for each of them, they are engaging in a collaborating style. The collaborating style mirrors the problem-solving model called The Standard Agenda discussed in chapter 8. By slightly changing the terminology of that model and applying it to conflict resolution, we get a six-step collaboration process:

1. **Define the problem**. Each party needs to identify that there is indeed a problem requiring attention.

2. **Explore the facts**. Both parties must identify their needs. Even more importantly, they must listen carefully to truly understand the needs of the other party. If you cannot get through

this step, collaboration cannot take place. Both parties must self-disclose honestly and completely.

3. **Brainstorm for possible solutions**. Generating as many solutions as possible and write them down.

4. **Set criteria to determine the best solution**. Generating a list of criteria that satisfies each person helps to determine the best solution. The first criterion should always be, "Any solution must be acceptable to both of us."

5. **Evaluate and select a solution**. Each solution is evaluated against the list of criteria to determine which solution might work best.

6. **Finally, test the solution**. Put the solution into action and see if it is effective.

Collaboration is very effective when each person needs to feel involved in resolving an issue. It does, however, take more time and communication than the other conflict-resolution styles.

Think about the number of people who must try to resolve conflicts with one another in the workplace. You can pick your romantic partner, but most often you don't get to pick your colleagues. How will you get along? There is no simple answer. Sometimes, two competitors will resent each other because no one can "win" the argument. We know two competitors, however, who get along well because they love to argue.

Putting a competitor in a relationship with an avoider may sound promising as a way to solve problems, but in reality it isn't. Think about people you know who use the competitive conflict-resolution style. How do they react when someone walks away from them? Most of them probably yell, [BOOMING] "DON'T YOU WALK AWAY FROM ME!" Two accommodators would get nowhere—"How do you want to format the report?" "I don't care. How do you want to format it?" "I don't care." What other combinations of conflict-resolution styles do you think would be particularly effective or ineffective?

Reflections on Conflict-Resolution Styles

It is important for you to think about your own style. Are you happy with it? Do you feel confident in your own conflict-resolution skills, or would you like to change? Anyone can learn these styles and use them, if they want to. But you also need to think a little about why you use your current style. Most traditional-age college students spent the last 20 years developing their style through interactions with their families and friends. Nontraditional students have spent even more time developing their style because they have life experiences in business and with families and friends.

If your personal style is to accommodate others, ask yourself whether you are doing this because you honestly don't have an opinion, you are very easygoing, or you were conditioned to use that style because of an abusive family situation. Children who grow up with alcoholic, drug-addicted, or verbally abusive parents learn very quickly to be accommodators so they can stay out of harm's way. However, you can change your style once you understand the reasons for your behavior.

If you are a competitor, you probably grew up in a family where arguments and discussions were openly encouraged. You not only were allowed to speak your mind but you were encouraged to do so. Think back to the discussion about the communication process. It is essential for you to understand the other person's circumstances in interpersonal communication—whether in a social or a business situation.

Let's look at the styles of coworkers, Nicole and Tiffany. Nicole grew up in an abusive family. Tiffany did not. When Tiffany wants to talk through a disagreement, Nicole simply acquiesces to Tiffany's viewpoint. Tiffany perceives Nicole as spineless with no opinion. With Tiffany's background, these characteristics are not desirable in her coworker. Nicole, on the other hand, is reminded of her abusive parent whenever Tiffany raises her voice and gets excited during a discussion. Once these colleagues talk about their personal circumstances (for example, their backgrounds), each of them can begin to alter their communication style. Altering their styles keeps the work relationship collegial. If they do not, the relationship may gradually fall apart. Even if Nicole and Tiffany are unwilling to change their styles, exploring their backgrounds should allow them a greater understanding of each other's style.

You may not always get to know your coworkers enough to gain an understanding of why they do what they do, but the effective use of the five styles of conflict resolution will help you smooth over conflict in work relationships. Since no style is appropriate in every situation, build your problem-solving skills so that you have options. You should practice using various styles in different situations. Having the knowledge and adaptability to use the appropriate style in each interpersonal situation helps you to become an effective communicator.

Even if you learn to use all of these styles effectively, it is important to remember there are some conflicts that can never be resolved completely. Sometimes, we are simply stuck working with people with whom we cannot get along; unpleasant people are part of the workforce. It may be necessary to keep your employment options open throughout your career so you never feel trapped. For example, working in a situation where a manager yells and screams at subordinates daily will be stressful, and you may dread going to work. Difficult work situations are simply that—difficult. Confidence in your own ability to communicate well helps you remain strong throughout the moments of conflict in your career. Maintaining a positive attitude allows you to move smoothly into a new career.

SEXUAL HARASSMENT

The workplace pays much more attention to sexual harassment today than it did 20 years ago. In fact, there really wasn't even a term for it 30 years ago or more. **Sexual harassment** is most often defined as "any unwanted sexual attention." If you think back to our previous discussions of communication, you're aware that attention can come in the form of verbal or nonverbal communication. And it comes in the form of intentional or unintentional communication. Your workplace should have a policy for sexual harassment, but we will mention a couple of specifics just to get you thinking about the topic.

Some departments and groups of colleagues develop their own communication culture. They function as a unique clique where language and images are used during communication without restrictions of any kind. For example, if you and a colleague use sexual jokes and innuendos, and you both enjoy them, you would not consider your communication sexual harassment. It doesn't fall under the definition of "unwanted." However, "Women tend to be more sensitive to offensive behavior, but it is unknown whether gender or other factors explain this higher sensitivity" (Young, Vance, and Ensher, 2003, p. 163). It's a wise idea to avoid the use of off-color material in a business setting until you know another person fairly well—and even then you risk violating company policy if someone overhears your remarks.

Verbal harassment includes suggestive remarks. A coworker may use paralanguage to make a remark fall under the definition of sexual harassment. There is nothing wrong with telling a colleague that he or she looks nice today, or that you like their outfit. However, certain paralanguage could make those same comments lecherous.

Try it in class. Have someone read the following statement in two different ways—once as a compliment and again with inflection that would qualify as sexual harassment: "Wow, you look really great today"

More blatant than suggestive remarks are outright sexual comments: commenting about body parts, telling sexual jokes, and making inappropriate invitations. Any requests that are quid pro quo (something for something) fall under this category also: "You will get promoted if you do X for me."

Nonverbal harassment can include any kind of inappropriate eye contact, gesture, touching, and so on. It is best to keep in mind the mantra you learned in kindergarten: Keep your hands to yourself. Brushing up against someone, if truly an isolated accident, is not a problem. If it happens repeatedly and it is unwanted, it is sexual harassment.

In addition to nonverbal gestures or facial movements, your artifacts may create a hostile environment. If office decorations make the workplace an uncomfortable place, that is a form of sexual harassment. It may be that someone displays a sexy calendar or poster that makes you uncomfortable. It may be that someone gives you a sexual gift (such as an adult magazine or product). Not everyone has the same sense of humor, and it is important not to cross these lines.

While you certainly need to address sexual harassment with the proper authorities, be certain that you have analyzed behaviors accurately. Communication can be intentional or unintentional, and we can sometimes resolve a misunderstanding by asking a question or alerting someone to the situation. Sometimes people are truly clueless that they are offending you. Below are some possible comments to consider:

"I'm not sure if you realize you are looking at my chest when you talk to me. Please look at my eyes when we are speaking."

"Would you be offended if I asked you to take down that poster?— it really makes me uncomfortable."

"I feel uncomfortable with that kind of language. Please don't use it around me."

Naturally you run the risk of the other party thinking you are overly sensitive. But no one should have to put up with sexual requests/language/jokes/pictures in the workplace if it makes them feel uncomfortable.

Be sure to follow your company's sexual harassment policy. Most policies begin by stating that you should clearly tell the offending person to stop the behavior. If that doesn't work, inform them in writing that you want the behavior stopped or you will alert authorities. If harassment continues, report it. One incident does not make a sexual harassment suit. There has to be a documented pattern of behavior. You should read the company's procedure regarding sexual harassment when you are hired initially. Then, you will know what to do if it happens.

PERFORMANCE REVIEWS

A **performance review** is a written document stating your strengths and weaknesses based on a manager's observation and analysis of your work. When you receive it, read it carefully and evaluate the information. If any of the statements in your review are incorrect or written in ambiguous language, ask your manager for a meeting and discuss the specifics. How can you improve your performance for the company if you do not know what a manager is criticizing? Address the inaccuracies by checking your documentation of messages, meetings, dates, etc. Since performance reviews are necessary in the workplace, you need to remember to keep meticulous records of everything you do from the moment you begin working for a company. Good record keeping makes the performance review process easier and less stressful because you can easily resolve inaccurate statements.

The review process is helpful because it lets you know how your communication and work is perceived by others. In many cases, it allows you to see if your interpersonal style is as effective as you think it is. Your daily social language and behavior as well as your ongoing business communication determine your value to the company. It is important to remain professional and credible the entire time you are working among peers. Ask your manager how you can improve if there are any negative statements in your review.

You should meet briefly with your manager to go over a performance review whether the material is positive or negative. Jennifer Becker, Jonathon Halbesleben, and Dan O'Hair (June, 2005) state, "Defensive communication can be minimized in such situations to the extent that supervisors focus on enhancing the strengths and future directions of the employee, for example by developing goal-setting strategies with the employee, rather than dwelling on past problematic behavior" (p. 149). The meeting to discuss a performance review allows you to demonstrate that you appreciate the time your manager took to write the document. At the same time, it gives you the opportunity to build a relationship with your manager as a thoughtful, concerned employee hopeful about your future with the organization. Always pay attention to the nonverbal behavior of the manager throughout the discussion so if you notice a reaction that does not match the words they are using you can ask for immediate clarification. Your ability to analyze the verbal and nonverbal aspects of interpersonal communication is truly critical for your survival in business. As a professional person, don't assume anything and make sure you understand everything clearly. It's difficult to improve if you aren't sure what a manager is asking you to do.

After your meeting with the manager, write a summary of the various points you discussed in the meeting and send it to him or her. Your written summary serves as an affirmation that you heard everything correctly and know how to proceed in your position until the next performance review. Excellent performance reviews will help you maintain morale throughout your working life. However, you are the one who must decide if there is a future for you with your current employer or if you should move on to fulfill your life's goal.

FINAL THOUGHTS

Employment would be much easier if you could hire yourself, make all of the decisions, take credit for everything that happens in the company, give yourself lavish bonuses, and live in a gated community with other people just like you. Sadly, a career doesn't work that way. A productive working life depends on excellent communication skills to assist you in maneuvering effortlessly with diverse colleagues as you make your way in the corporate world. Those same communication skills are also used to face and conquer the challenging moments of employment reflected in personal conflict, sexual harassment, and performance reviews. Challenging moments in communication and behavior allow you to demonstrate your personal credibility as a professional person. Your image management during cycles of tense communication reflects your value and maturity to a company.

The concepts in this chapter are easy to interpret as moments that happen due to the actions of others. In other words, you need to be aware of how to handle situational conflict, how to react to sexual harassment, and how to handle a performance review in a professional manner. These assumptions are true, but it is also true that communication occurs between two or more people. This means that your personal language and behavior may be the cause of the challenging situations you find yourself in occasionally. Analyzing your own communication first is an excellent way to approach problem solving. Once you understand potential communication errors you may have made, you can more accurately discover solutions to resolve a conflict with a colleague or manager, a sexually uncomfortable confrontation, and clarify factual/perceptual language in a performance review. You are a partner in every communication exchange and must accept responsibility for your actions just as colleagues need to accept responsibility for their actions. Professionalism requires constant use of appropriate language and behavior with others.

KEY TERMS

Accommodating	Interest conflicts
Avoiding	Moral conflicts
Bullying	Performance review
Collaborating	Relationship conflicts
Competing	Sexual harassment
Compromising	Structural conflicts
Conflict	Value conflicts
Data conflicts	Withdrawing

EXERCISES

1. Describe a conflict situation you experienced and the personal style you used at the time. How would you change your communication now?

2. Describe a situation in which you experienced or observed sexual harassment. What did you do at the time? How would you handle it now?

3. Write a personal performance review of your work (attendance, written work, class participation) up to this point in the term. How can you improve your professional image before the end of the term?

11

Good Things to Know Something About

After reading this chapter you should be able to:

✓ Differentiate between networks and networking

✓ Describe how you can use storytelling in the workplace

✓ Explain key differences in masculine and feminine communication

✓ Explain the implications of working with people from different cultures

✓ Identify effective strategies for dining out

There are a variety of interpersonal issues that you will encounter as your career begins. These issues ebb and flow throughout your working life. Hard work alone does not solidify a career. Your peers and managers constantly evaluate you for your ability to communicate in a responsible manner as well as for your earning potential to the employer. Therefore, it is useful to know something about the additional interpersonal scenarios mentioned in this chapter. Some of the scenarios require your time away from work and family. You are expected to remain current in your field throughout your career in addition to representing the company with outside interests and activities. There is no better time than now to begin thinking about a professional way of life and how to effectively use communication opportunities to remain relevant for employment.

NETWORKS AND NETWORKING

Networks are comprised of individuals with similar philosophical thoughts, personal goals, or belief systems. They consist of professional organizations, nonprofit organizations, corporations, religious groups, unions, fraternal societies, support groups, neighborhood organizations, and so on. Connecting to people and keeping in touch with them is a way to share thoughts, ideas, job opportunities, and promotions.

Whereas people once networked via a contraption called a Rolodex (where you physically recorded the name and contact information of people you had met), networking is a much easier concept with the advent of electronic social networking venues such as Facebook and LinkedIn. Facebook and Twitter have expanded rapidly and are often used in the business world today. Many businesses have daily Tweets to connect to consumers and employees. New networks spring up daily. For example, Quora was the idea of two former Facebook engineers. Although it drew fewer than 200,000 monthly visitors in early 2011, the site for posting questions and searching among the answers attracts CEOs from Silicon Valley. "So why is Quora attracting so much attention? It's the community. . . . Everybody seems to be of above-average intelligence, often with an above-average stake in the subject" (McCracken, 2011). That was the assessment at the time we were writing this text. By the time you read this book, it will be interesting to see whether this network has blossomed.

Susan Nan describes networks as "social structures that connect people to each other" and "in connecting people or organizations, networks allow activities that no individual or organization could accomplish single-handedly" (2008, p. 113). There are inclusive and exclusive networks. Inclusive networks allow anyone to join, and exclusive networks do not. Inclusive networks are useful in conflict resolution, while exclusive networks can entrench conflict. According to Nan, some of the benefits of networks in resolving conflicts are:

- Increased access to information, expertise, and financial resources
- Increased efficiency
- Multiplier effect (increases the reach and impact to member organizations)
- Solidarity and support
- Increased visibility of issues, best practices, and underrepresented groups
- Increased credibility
- Risk regulation
- Reduced isolation (p. 117)

Networks also develop within organizations as a function of structure and hierarchy. You work daily with colleagues at your level of the company. This communication creates a bond between you. Though you communicate with your supervisor as necessary and with other company employees at different levels, your most immediate contacts are the colleagues who hold a similar title to your own.

A supervisor is above you in the company hierarchy, so suggestions and complaints are forwarded to that person. In a company with a vertical hierarchy structure, you forward information and ideas to your immediate supervisor; you do not bypass that level to reach a higher managerial level. Forwarding ideas to individuals above your supervisor without his or her knowledge is unprofessional and often considered an act of defiance. An error in corporate protocol can be costly.

Staff communication is a daily activity also. Administrative assistants, custodial engineers, and dining room personnel are referred to as staff positions and you deal with all of them in addition to colleagues and your boss. Your communication with all staff members must be cordial and professional. Some individuals consider staff employees as inferiors and are occasionally rude to them. Not only is such behavior insulting, but it does not convey a favorable image of you to observers. You should be professional with every person in the corporate environment to maintain a credible image.

Networking is a cumulative action. It requires a portion of your mental and personal time. At the beginning of your career, you will spend a lot of your personal time networking with individuals and organizations as you demonstrate to others that you have the passion and interest for a long-term career. The following are a few suggestions to help you make the most of networking opportunities.

- Be curious about the company. Meet people in every area of the company to deepen your understanding of how the business works. These visits make people notice you and recognize that you are interested in the company as a whole rather than limited to selfish interests. The visits also broaden your understanding of the career opportunities within your own company so you can make informed decisions about growth and advancement.

- Be polite to everyone you meet. The professional world is smaller than you realize, and you never know who belongs to what network. Connections drive careers, so make sure everyone who meets you has a positive experience and remembers your name.

- Attend some of the after-work social functions. This is a great way to unwind and talk to colleagues in a social setting. These sessions can build strong social bonds. You do not have to drink alcohol to be in a social setting. Bars serve ginger ale and club soda, so go and have some fun. If you do indulge, do so carefully. In larger cities, every business and even the management levels within businesses hang out in specific bars or restaurants. Being in those environments may give you an opportunity to meet people. Over time, you can make better decisions about which individuals can make your "good-colleagues-to-know" list. Employees change companies and advance in rank, so it's important to keep an eye on your own future.

- Find a way to remain in touch with people you like throughout your career. Everyone uses a different way to keep in touch with important people, so find a method that works for you and never lose touch with key people.

- Join professional and community organizations as a volunteer. The activity builds work experience away from the company and gives you new contacts and ideas for self-development. Listen as others are talking about the organizations and join those organizations that have the potential to promote your career. Sometimes the contacts you make can be useful should you choose to change careers or are downsized from current employment. Every contact you make can be valuable to you.

- Remain up-to-date on all of the literature and analysis in your professional area of expertise: nationally and internationally. The information allows you to participate in social conversations at work and demonstrates your interest in the future of the company.

- Remain active in activities you enjoy; those experiences will also help you contribute to informal conversations at work. A large majority of business personnel talk about various sports teams, so if sports trivia is a passion of yours—terrific. However, business colleagues also meet socially to play various sports such as golf, tennis, racquetball, etc. If you play any of these sports, you might be invited to join other colleagues and begin to feel included in those groups, too. There are other passions professional people like to discuss such as literature, coaching young people in the community, training seniors to use the computer to stay connected to the outside world, and so on. The key to any interest you possess is your commitment to reach out to others and the length of time you've been connected to the activity. Numerous interests make you of "value" to the business sector.

- If someone goes out on a professional limb to give you the contact information of a trusted colleague, keep the name, address, and phone number of that person, and other trusted contacts, in a private place no one else can access. If possible, never store their information anywhere (cell phone data can be accessed by others or lost). Above all, do not "reshare" those contacts with others. These individuals are your contacts only, so protect their privacy. And be sure to remain in touch with them for advice, mentoring, and information throughout your life.

Networking requires time and additional financial resources for food, beverages, and commuting. The expansion of your knowledge base and career contacts makes the investment a wise one. The more individuals who know you personally, the more likely someone will alert you to possibilities for advancement. Networks can make a tremendous difference in your satisfaction with your professional life.

STORYTELLING IN INTERPERSONAL SETTINGS

Storytelling skills are an excellent tool to use in business to boost morale, deliver information, and assist others in understanding new concepts. This device allows you to be more creative during presentations because adjectives and adverbs are used more frequently to present colorful images to the audience. **Storytelling** usually involves an emotional description of time, events, action, and places that translates factual information into life experiences that audience members have in common and will remember. The oral traditions of many cultures include stories, which present messages of hope, stewardship, ethical behavior, leadership, and problem solving. The key to good storytelling is a thorough understanding of the audience and the common experiences and beliefs they share. You simply mold the story to a business model.

John Brown and Paul Duguid (2000) advocate telling stories in the workplace to promote organizational learning, increase employee intelligence, and boost innovation. They refer to the use of stories as "social software." Clive Muir (2007) believes instructors, trainers, consultants, and others can teach students and employees to turn their stories into "instruments for personal, professional, and organizational success" (p. 369).

Strong work experience and life experience becomes the background for the stories you develop. You, family members, friends and/or an organization itself become the characters used in the message you create. When an audience believes you are tied to the tale, they are more likely to listen to what you are saying. This creative speaking style is completely different from the factual presentational style normally used in business. It can't be used in all corporate scenarios but when appropriate, storytelling becomes a refreshing, effective way to exchange information with others and to motivate them, as well as to be remembered.

GENDER COMMUNICATION

Speech patterns refer to the way a particular group of people communicates. Extensive research in the field of **gender communication** has revealed that men and women typically have different and distinct communication patterns. This is no surprise if you have fought with someone of the opposite sex or been frustrated by the way they spoke to you.

There are numerous books on this topic, and we recommend *Gendered Lives* by Julia Wood and *You Just Don't Understand* and *Talking from 9 to 5* by Deborah Tannen if you want an in-depth look at some differences in gender communication. We'll briefly review some helpful tips for familiarizing yourself with gendered communication in the workplace.

There are masculine and feminine speech styles. The styles usually correspond with men and women, but not always, and the language styles are changing rapidly. Why? Some gender theories trace patterns of communication to the games that people play when they are young. Boys, in general, play sports, and when they go out to play, there is not much talking necessary regarding the rules of the game. Everyone knows what to do, and they do it. The goal is to win. Girls, in general, enact social situations (playing school, playing house). In this game, they do a lot of talking to negotiate how the game will be played. And there is no "winning" in these types of games. The goal is to discuss, to create scenarios, and to enjoy one another's company.

Growing up with distinct models of communication influences adult speech patterns. In other words, men, in general, talk when it is absolutely necessary, talk to win, and are very directive. Women, in general, talk more often, talk to enjoy one another's company, to build relationships, and to be inclusive in their communication.

Gender communication theories are evolving as girls' behavior changes. Girls now play more sports and develop mechanical skills as quickly as boys. The women in our classes who played sports with the boys typically possess more masculine speech qualities than women who played exclusively with dolls and weren't physically active when they were kids. And boys brought up with more creative play often have the ability to exhibit the more supportive/inclusive style of speaking.

Brenda Allen (2011) makes the point that organizations themselves are gendered.

> The gendered nature of organizations is evident in many communication practices, policies, and preferences. Women and men learn to conform to formal expectations or unspoken norms about aspects of appearance, such as types of clothing, grooming, and acceptable body weight. Many, if not most, of these policies and norms persist without challenge and are based on masculinist, white, middle-class and middle-age ideals and aesthetics. (p. 56)

Feminine styles of communication—inclusive, collaborating, and cooperating—are often linked with subordinate roles in the organization. Organizational structure often includes hierarchies and chains of command, similar to the military. Organizations tend to value masculine ways of communicating. "A masculine ethic of reason and rationality underpins images of professionalism in organizations. . . . Ideas of professionalism usually encompass masculine ways of being, including assertion, independence, competitiveness, confidence, competition, domination, and winning" (Allen, p. 57).

Allen notes that we produce, reproduce—and sometimes challenge and change—expectations and stereotypes about gender in organizational contexts.

Wood (2011) talks about specific and harmful stereotypes for both women and men in corporate culture. Women are stereotyped as:

- *Sex object*—defining her by her looks rather than by her accomplishments

- *Mother*—acting as though she is supposed to take care of everyone

- *Child*—treating her as though she needs to be taken care of

- *Iron maiden*—stereotyping an "independent, ambitious, directive, and competitive" woman in an extremely negative light

Obviously these stereotypes are not flattering and they encourage workers to treat women as less than equals. The male stereotypes are equally troubling. Men are stereotyped as:

- *Sturdy oak*—expecting the man to always be strong and self-reliant

- *Fighter*—expecting the man to take charge and fight all of the battles

- *Breadwinner*—judging a man on his abilities as the wage earner (pp. 230–234)

While these stereotypes are not as demeaning as some of the female stereotypes, they limit men's abilities to show an emotional or sensitive side, to take advantage of paternity leaves, or stay home to care for sick children. They also impose a negative stigma for a man whose wife is employed in a position where she earns more money.

Keep these cautions in mind while considering the following scenario at work. He comes in and gets right to the task that needs to be done. She wants to talk a little about the day, ask how things are going, etc. These two people annoy each other. She nods and says "uh huh" during the time he is talking. She is showing inclusiveness and encouragement for him to keep talking; he is annoyed by the interruption. When he communicates with her on the phone, he simply listens while she talks. He does not interject a reinforcing "uh-huh" or "ok." She gets angry at the silence assuming that he is not listening to her. Their perceptions of each other could be corrected by understanding different communication styles. The gender roles learned in childhood need to be tempered so that communication is more effective and all employees can feel at ease while contributing to common goals. Excellent communication skills and intelligence are not restricted to one gender. Talent, credibility, and leadership are genderless traits.

INTERCULTURAL COMMUNICATION

Today's workplaces are comprised of individuals from different ethnic, religious, social, and educational backgrounds, necessitating an awareness of different communication patterns across cultures, which is the focus of **intercultural communication**. It is important to remember that people from other cultures will interact in communication situations according to the patterns they learned—which may well differ from the patterns you learned. This statement may sound obvious. However, it is easy to forget cultural differences. For example, if an individual speaks English flawlessly with no accent, we may automatically assume that all other aspects of the individual's approach to interactions will match our own. Yet, nonverbal behaviors such as approach to time have nothing to do with proficiency in English as a second language. If someone does not meet your expectations, cultural differences may be the cause rather than a perceived deficiency.

Working with people from diverse backgrounds occasionally requires some language and behavioral problem-solving skills. Try to analyze the cultural nuances before reaching any conclusions about the other person. For instance, Americans tend to get straight to business while Mexicans tend to want to talk a little bit about their families before they get started. People from India may say they can do a task, even if they can't. They view this verbal reaction to a speaker as being polite—similar to Americans who nod their head while someone is speaking to them as a polite way to signal nonverbally that they are listening. So for someone from India, it is polite to say that they can finish a 50-page report by tomorrow, even if it is impossible to complete the task.

Touch is one of the areas of nonverbal communication that varies tremendously from one culture to the next. You need to be perceived as professional when you travel, so it is useful to know how to greet business colleagues on an international business meeting. A little research before you travel can assist you in knowing what to do so you make a good impression for your company.

Corporate employment involves global culture. Even if you don't travel for an international division of a company, you will probably participate in a virtual meeting with global colleagues. You need to constantly inform yourself about the cultural traditions of colleagues as well as employers to avoid communication mistakes that can be costly

A handshake is considered to be an international business greeting but varies from culture to culture, so it is important to adopt the appropriate greeting. In Australia, a man will not reach for a woman's hand because he does not want to be physically demonstrative with the woman. In China, the preferred handshake is very light and not forceful. Sometimes a bow or slight nod is the most useful greeting. When greeting in France, a kiss is preferred even if the encounter is brief. The number of kisses varies depending on the region. Even regions close to the United States geographically have significant differences in their greetings. Canadians will offer their hand but stand much closer than Americans feel comfortable, and the man will wait for a woman to offer her hand first. It is important to know the preferred greeting of a culture to establish comfort and trust in the relationship (Kienzle and Husar, 2007, pp. 83–84).

to your career and costly to your employer. Natalie Kienzle and Shane Husar (2007) state, "Cultural intelligence is defined as being skilled and flexible about understanding a culture, learning increasingly more about it, and gradually shaping one's thinking to be more sympathetic to the culture and one's behavior to be more fine-tuned and appropriate when interacting with others from the culture" (p. 84). They list five stages involved in developing cultural intelligence:

1. Reactivity to external stimuli.

2. Recognition of other cultural norms and motivation to learn more about them.

3. Accommodation of other cultural norms and rules.

4. Assimilation of diverse cultural norms into alternative behaviors.

5. Pro-activity in cultural behavior based on recognition of changing cues that others do not perceive. (p. 84)

Cultural competence refers to your ability to interact effectively with people from other cultures—understanding and accepting the beliefs, values, and ethics of others plus developing the skills necessary to work with diverse individuals. Allen (2011) highlights the following four components of cultural competence.

- *Awareness*. Examine your own cultural background, including values and prejudices. Become aware of the impact of culture on your life and of how you perceive and respond to other cultures.

- *Attitude*. Respect others. Be sensitive to and open-minded about cultural differences.

- *Knowledge*. Recognize power structures and institutional barriers that prevent individuals from using organizational resources.

- *Skills*. Develop and improve verbal and nonverbal cross-cultural communication skills.

"By becoming culturally competent, you learn more about yourself as well as others, thereby expanding your horizons and gaining a better understanding of multiple views and experiences that form the foundation from which others see the world" (Allen, 2011, p. 75).

Today's technology allows you to communicate instantly around the world. To stand out in your profession, you must be knowledgeable in how to use language effectively with individuals from other cultures and adapt to new behaviors. Cultural intelligence is important to develop as the finances of the corporate world mingle to a greater extent than at any other time in world history.

THE ART OF BUSINESS DINING

As Dana Casperson (2001) notes: "More than half of all business deals are finalized over a meal and a higher percentage of business discussion in general occurs while out to lunch or dinner" (p. 68). It may seem odd to talk about eating in a communication book. However, long gone are the days when parents required perfect table manners at home and took children to elegant teas and restaurants to learn the fine art of dining. Many job offers and business deals are conducted at a dining table. Therefore, a little etiquette information becomes useful knowledge. Some of you may know the following information, but many students are clueless on how to conduct themselves when it comes to eating at restaurants other than fast-food or casual, family-style establishments.

Casperson (2001) provides a brief do and don't list.

- Avoid talking with food in your mouth

- Give your dining companion full attention

- Turn off your cell phone

- Keep absences brief

- Steer clear of inappropriate discussions
- Don't interrupt
- Avoid alcoholic beverages
- Avoid messy foods (p. 68)

A few of these items are worthy of further comment. Obviously if you must use the restroom or make a call, keep it very brief. You should not leave your dinner companion alone, particularly if the person is your superior. But let's be honest about human physiology; there are those rare and unfortunate events that occur with our bodily systems. If you know you will be in the bathroom for a while, it may be best to excuse yourself with "Would you excuse me? I'm terribly sorry, but I may be a little while." That gives the other person a head's up not to worry if you aren't back in the normal time frame for a table departure.

While Casperson says to avoid alcohol, we would argue that moderation, if acceptable in your company, is certainly appropriate. There are some bosses who do not like to drink alone and feel a little miffed if you don't join them for a cocktail. You will have to judge this issue one meal at a time and know your limit! However, if you don't drink, don't compromise. There is nothing wrong with ordering a club soda or simply drinking water.

It is wise to avoid ordering messy or hard to eat foods. No club sandwiches or huge burgers that you can't bite easily. Sloppy sauces look great on the plate but not on your clothing. If you order a salad with huge chunks of lettuce, spend some time cutting it up before attempting to eat it. Choosing a large salad during a business lunch/dinner may mean that you are still eating when everyone else is finished. Visualize what family members look like eating various items. Those images will assist you in choosing wisely from the menu when sitting across the table from your boss or a client.

The person who invites another person(s) to dine out is the host for the event. Casperson (2001) identifies the duties of a host and guest. Host duties include personally extending the invitation, making the reservation, arriving early, creating atmosphere, and deciding when to bring up serious discussion. Guest duties include confirming the meeting, arriving on time, coming prepared, being prepared to pay if necessary, and sending a thank-you note.

Lydia Ramsey (2004) also shares some tips for a successful business meeting while dining out:

- Plan ahead. Issue the invitations one week ahead for a dinner and three days for a lunch. Always double check your schedule to ensure you haven't overbooked yourself.

- Confirm the meal with your client.

- Arrive early.

- Seat the guests strategically. When dining with one client, sit to his or her right. With more than one client, seat in order of importance: don't put the people you'll be talking to the most on either side of you or you won't be able to pay attention to both. Sit one next to you and the other across from you.

- Allow your guests to order first.

- Keep an eye on the time.

- Limit your consumption of alcohol. (pp. 22–23)

Ramsey makes an excellent point about the time limit. Lunches shouldn't be open-ended. And it is up to the host to close the meeting. Just as in a speech or other type of meeting, the host needs to conclude gracefully and let people get back to the office.

While it is absolutely proper manners to have your guests order first, it is uncomfortable as a guest to order and then find out everyone else gets something much less expensive. Aim for the middle to lower price end of the menu if you are the guest. For instance, if entrées run from $12–35, shoot for something around $15–18. If you find that you've made a huge faux pas when your boss orders something far smaller, there is nothing wrong with saying, "Oh I didn't see that—I think I'd like that instead." If you are the host, put your guests at ease. As Ramsey notes:

> Your conduct over the meal will determine your professional success. If you pay attention to the details and make every effort to see that your clients have a pleasant experience, they will assume that you handle your business the same way. (2004, p. 23)

As you can see from the protocol outlined above, there are definite business rules of etiquette to follow for anyone issuing an invitation to dine out.

Guests are expected to behave in a professional fashion. Therefore, the casual offer to have lunch with someone may not be so casual after all. Even in this seemingly relaxed eating environment, there are interpersonal rules of conduct for professional people.

FINAL THOUGHTS

The concepts mentioned in this chapter are a reminder to perfect interpersonal skills for the challenges faced in a successful working career. You may feel you have the skills and knowledge to do a job well, but you need to measure your opinion versus the impressions of other people, who will continually assess your personal credibility and your value to the organization. Your career path is inescapably linked to the perceptions others make about your talent. Other people open the door for your career and its sustainability. The manner in which you perform work tasks is as important as the tasks themselves, and requires vigilance on your part: networks need constant monitoring; storytelling makes you an interesting, valued colleague; knowledge about gendered communication will aid your interactions with others; cultural intelligence makes a great impression on everyone; and respectful, informed dining etiquette reveals your social skills. Sound judgment and excellent communication skills create employees that add value to an organization.

Throughout this book, we have highlighted certain behaviors and asked whether they were appropriate. You make ethical decisions daily; as a member of an organization, your behavior will impact colleagues. Patricia Andrews and John Baird (2005) address the question of why it is important to behave ethically if unethical behavior might provide a competitive advantage professionally. They point out that honesty in business dealings creates an environment of trust, which is essential for organizations to function effectively. Trust is a fundamental requirement for communities, organizations, and societies. "Knowing that you are honest, that you behave humanely in your dealings with your fellow employees, that you are fair in your evaluations of others, and that you are concerned for the welfare of the whole organization and the society it serves are important self-perceptions that truly are priceless" (p. 6). If you behave ethically, the people with whom you work are more likely to engage in ethical behavior. Conversely, unethical behavior can have serious ramifications. Unethical practices affect everyone; companies fail and employees lose their livelihood when reputations are ruined because of unethical behavior.

Personal development continues throughout your lifetime. Work experience becomes your greatest ally when seeking employment because practical experience captures the attention of employers. Once you develop your intrapersonal strengths and skills, your ability to communicate well and adapt to new business opportunities guide your future path. Some new employment opportunities will be driven by new technology and global finance. In addition, your working life will probably involve interactions with people from other countries and new cultures. It is easy to adapt to change even though it may seem awkward at first. You must understand yourself thoroughly and what motivates you to establish a life-long career. Who are you? What do you want? Establish a personal brand that displays confidence; be the type of person with whom other people enjoy working. Consistent communication throughout your working life will provide answers to the philosophical questions you currently ask yourself regarding your ability and worth to the corporate world. Employment is challenging, but with constant monitoring of your communication and behavioral skills, it is also extremely rewarding.

> Do not go where the path may lead. Go instead where there is no path and leave a trail.
>
> —Ralph Waldo Emerson

KEY TERMS

Cultural competence	Networking
Gender communication	Networks
Intercultural communication	Storytelling

EXERCISES

1. Describe your networking strategy to gain employment or attend graduate school.
2. Conduct an informative interview with a foreign student. Ask the interviewee to describe the language and behavioral differences between his or her culture and American culture. What did you learn that you can apply to your professional life?
3. How does your behavior and attitude change when working for a male versus female manager or teacher? Why?

Additional Resources

New employees may have a number of questions that are not covered in the employee manual. Here are some questions you might have and some suggestions for handling common situations, as well as sources to explore for more information.

How do I accomplish the huge task that my boss just handed to me?

One of the best ways to attempt to keep yourself from becoming overwhelmed is to "break challenging projects or activities into smaller parts and work on one part at a time. When you have accomplished one, move on to the next." Retrieved from http://msn.careerbuilder.com/Article/MSN-2379-Job-Search-Lacking-Confidence-That-May-Be-the-Reason-Youre-Still-Job-Searching/?SiteId=cbmsnhp42379&sc_extcmp=JS_2379_home1&gt1=23000

How do I keep moving forward in my career?

One of the keys is to always have a list of goals. What do you want to accomplish in your career history? List your short- and long-term goals, both in your career and personal life, and a time line for achieving them; also write down action steps to achieve your goals. The lists and time line will help you remain focused, rather than letting time slip away. Retrieved from http://msn.careerbuilder.com/Article/MSN-2379-Job-Search-Lacking-Confidence-That-May-Be-the-Reason-Youre-Still-Job-Searching/?SiteId=cbmsnhp42379&sc_extcmp=JS_2379_home1&gt1=23000

I am so angry about something that happened at work. Can I let my friends know about it on Facebook?

Steve Daily, Associate Producer with Fox Sports South and one of our alums, says, "Don't broadcast it: Don't go on your Facebook page and post anything about the company that you work for, especially something negative. Companies monitor these websites now and check up on what their employees are saying. If you put on your twitter page that the VP really annoyed you today with his long speech, he could be reading that in the next few days. Keep those profiles on a private setting. Eliminate those tags on photos of you doing shots from back in college. You might think, hey it was a long time ago. Your boss doesn't know that. Finally, don't use media sites while you are on the clock unless it is part of your job! If you post that you are bored at work, you just told your boss 'I'm not working.'"

I'm not really up on the latest technology of tweets, social networking, apps, etc. Do I really need to know this stuff?

Sadly, yes. Numerous businesses are using apps and twitter as well as social networking sites to drive business their way. If you don't know how to use these sources of communication, you are going to be left behind for someone who does. A fascinating article even talks about how libraries (remember those quiet places where you go to read?) are "tweeting, texting, and launching smart-phone apps as they try to keep up with the bibliotechs—a computer-savvy class of people who consider card catalogs as vintage as typewriters." Retrieved from http://www.usatoday.com/tech/news/2010-10-03-library-ipod_N.htm

How do I get my dream job?

Joanie Cole Berney writes, "Is there really a dream job? To me a dream job is a job that you love doing. I love what I do, so I guess you could say I have a dream job.

"After staying at home with my two daughters for many years, I decided to return to the workforce full time. Most women will agree that being out of the workforce for a few months—let alone a few years—can make it hard to return. I heard that the local sports and entertainment arena was in the need for a receptionist. Now, this sports and entertainment facility was only a few years old and I had only been to a few of the concerts there. In fact, the first time I went to a concert there, I walked in, handed the ticket taker my ticket and thought to myself: I want to work here. Never did I think I would be doing what I do now, but I knew I wanted to work in that building. I got an interview for that receptionist position and was offered the job.

"Believe it or not, I actually turned the job down. In my mind it was almost like that receptionist job was a bit beneath me. At my age I thought I should be able to do better; did I really want to be tied down to a desk and answer phones all day? The minute I turned the job down, I regretted it. I felt I had made one of the worst mistakes of my life. Well, I have never been one to burn bridges or give up, so I contacted the arena and told them I had made a terrible mistake in turning down the position and if the person they hired instead of me didn't work out to keep me in mind. Months passed and I forgot about the position. Sure, I would see an ad for a concert and think to myself, I could be working there—but life went on. One day out of the blue, the arena called and said that the person they hired for the reception position left and if I wanted the position this time, it was mine.

"I did not hesitate at all and accepted the position. This time I looked at the receptionist position as a foot in the door, and once I got in that door there was no telling where it could lead me. I offered to help people in other departments when they were busy. I took on the tasks that weren't getting done or that no one else wanted to do. I made that reception position a professional position; I took pride in answering those calls. I always had a smile on my face. It paid off. At my first yearly review I was told I was the best receptionist they ever had. I was given more and more responsibility and moved from the receptionist to the website coordinator to the marketing assistant to the current position I have now—marketing coordinator. I hope someday the opportunity arises for me to be the director of marketing at the building I am currently at or maybe even another building.

"I have always told my daughters and the interns who work for me that there is nothing wrong with having a dream or a goal. It is good to set goals for yourself, and if you don't reach those goals right away, don't give up. Take each job you have and make the most of it. Never lose contact with people; you never know when you might need them. Always be friendly and helpful and willing to give 100%. No one remembers that person who frowned all the time; they remember the person with the smile on their face who made sure to say good morning to them everyday.

"I can honestly say I look forward to going to work each day. I don't know if there are a lot of people in the world who can really say that. Do I have the perfect job? No. Would I like to make more money? Yes. Would I take a job that I hated if it paid more than the one I have now? No. For me to be truly happy, I have to do what I love. I love promoting concerts. I love working with media outlets. I love the inner workings of the entertainment world. I love, love, love a show day! I love when the artist takes the stage and the crowd goes wild. In my eyes I have found my dream job. Will I be at this job forever? Who really can see into the future like that? For right now, I just enjoy doing the best that I can at a job that I truly love."

I've only seen old-looking formats for résumés. Is there anything that would set me apart?

Yes, we've come across a new source called www.blueskyresumes.com that offers a number of different formats for different professions. We think it is a terrific new way to explore visual formats that may be different from what you've seen in the past.

I just started working at a company and I really enjoy my coworkers. The problem is that every time I turn around I'm being asked for a gift donation. There is a cake fund for birthdays, holiday gifts for cleaning people, shower gifts for new babies, etc. I don't want to be a spoil-sport, but my budget is extremely tight. What are the expectations?

This is a tough problem. It is no fun eating beans for diner while shelling out large amounts of money for "unnecessary" items—when you could be using that money to pay the electric bill. On the other hand, when an employee refuses to donate, the gesture does not go unnoticed. You might see if you can contribute a lesser amount. In the long run, you have to figure out which consequence is worse—being perceived as a non-contributor or cutting back more on your own spending. If you plead poverty, make sure you don't parade around your new iPhone or talk about the latest item you purchased. Sometimes it is best to just chalk up the donations as the price of being employed—not unlike needing proper attire and transportation.

My boss is touching me on the shoulders, and I don't like it. What should I do?

If the behavior happens again, immediately respond by saying, "Please don't touch me. Thanks." If the behavior continues, consult with your HR department if there is one and/or put your concern in writing. If the pattern continues, then it is time to get legal advice.

What kind of interview questions should I expect?

Here are some of the top questions we have found:

1. Where would you like to be in your career five years from now?
2. Tell me about your proudest achievement.
3. Give me an example of a time when you had to think outside the box.
4. What negative thing would your last boss say about you?
5. What can you do for us that other candidates can't?
6. What are the responsibilities of your current or previous position?
7. What do you know about this industry?
8. What do you know about our company?
9. How long will it take for you to make a significant contribution?
10. What is your most significant accomplishment?
11. Why did you leave your last job?
12. Why do you think you would like to work for our company?
13. If it were your first day, what would you say to the associates you will be working with?
14. What have you done to overcome major obstacles in your life?
15. Are you willing to relocate?
16. How would you describe your work style?
17. Tell me about yourself.
18. Why do you think we should hire you for this job?
19. How do you define success?
20. What was the last book you read?
21. What area of this job would you find most difficult?
22. What leadership/supervisory roles have you held?
23. What is your weakness?
24. What accomplishments are you most proud of?
25. What has been your greatest crisis, how did you solve it?

26. What person has had the greatest influence on you, why?

27. What do you like best about your job/school . . . what do you like least?

28. How has college prepared you for this career?

29. Describe your ideal job.

30. Why did you choose this particular field of work?

31. What have you done that shows initiative?

32. In what areas of the job would you expect to be most successful . . . least successful?

33. What are your salary requirements?

34. What frustrates you?

35. Describe a situation with an irate customer and how you handled it.

36. What aspect of this job do you consider most crucial?

37. What are your long-range career objectives and how do you plan to achieve them?

38. How do you think a friend would describe you?

39. What motivates you?

40. How many hours a week do you need to work to get the job done?

41. How do you work under pressure?

42. What two or three things are most important to you in your job?

43. Tell me about other jobs you've had. In hindsight, how could you have improved your performance?

44. What makes a good supervisor?

45. What skills do you want to improve?

46. What qualities do you look for in a boss?

47. What have you learned from mistakes on the job? What experience do you have in this field?

48. What motivates you to do your best on the job? Do you consider yourself successful?

49. What do coworkers say about you?

50. What has disappointed you about a job?

51. Tell me about a problem you had with a supervisor.

52. Are you a team player?

53. Have you ever had to fire anyone? How did you feel about that?

54. What is your philosophy toward work?

55. Explain how you would be an asset to this organization.

56. What would your previous supervisor say your strongest point is?

57. Tell me about a suggestion you have made.

58. What irritates you about coworkers?

59. Describe your management style.

60. What is your greatest strength?

61. Tell me about your dream job.

62. What kind of person would you refuse to work with?

63. Why do you think you would do well at this job?

64. How do you propose to compensate for your lack of experience?

65. Tell me about a time when you helped resolve a dispute between others.

66. Describe your work ethic.

67. What has been your biggest professional disappointment?

68. Tell me about the most fun you have had on the job.

69. How do you react to negativity or gossip from coworkers?

70. If you were unable to meet a commitment or deadline, what would you do?

71. Do you prefer to work alone or in a group?

72. What have I forgotten to ask?

References

Allen, B. (2011). *Difference Matters: Communicating Social Identity*, 2nd ed. Long Grove, IL: Waveland Press, Inc.

Andersen, P. A. (2008). *Nonverbal Communication: Forms and Functions*, 2nd ed. Long Grove, IL: Waveland Press, Inc.

Andrews, P. H., and J. E. Baird. (2005). *Communication for Business and the Professions*, 8th ed. Long Grove, IL: Waveland Press, Inc.

Associated Press. (2006, August 31). "RadioShack Fires 400 by E-mail." Retrieved from http://www.seattlepi.com/business/283213_emaillayoffs31.html

Baird, J. (2010, January 28). "An Unquiet Nation." Retrieved from http://www.newsweek.com/id/232668/output/print)

Bambacas, M., and M. Patrickson. (2008). "Interpersonal Communication Skills that Enhance Organizational Commitment." *Journal of Communication Management*, 12 (1), pp. 51–72.

Becker, J. A. H., J. R. B. Halbesleben, and H. D. O'Hair. (2005). "Defensive Communication and Burnout in the Workplace: The Mediating Role of Leader-Member Exchange." *Communication Research Reports*, 22 (2), pp. 143–150.

Bennett, J. (2010, November 1). "Privacy Is Dead." *Newsweek*, pp. 40–41.

Bens, I. (May–July, 2008). "Seven Guiding Principles." *Dispute Resolution Journal*, 63 (2), p. 91.

Brown, J. S., and P. Duguid. (2000). *The Social Life of Information*. Boston: Harvard Business School Press.

Burns, J. M. (1978). *Leadership*. New York: Harper & Row.

"Candidate Interview Questions." Retrieved from http://career.mansfield.edu/media/files/Candidate%20Interview%20Questions%20%2D%20website.pdf

Casperson, D. (2001). "Mastering the Business Meal." *Training & Development*, 55(3), p. 68.

Chaleff, I. (2009). *The Courageous Follower: Standing Up To and For Our Leaders*. San Francisco: Berrett-Koehler Publishers.

Croal, N. (2008, June 16). "Thoughtcasting: UR So Vain." *Newsweek*, p. 56.

Davis, D. A. C., and N. M. Scaffidi. (2007, May). Leading Virtual Teams. Paper presented to the 56th annual convention of the International Communication Association (Organizational Communication Division), San Francisco, CA.

Dehne, S. (2010). "Lacking Confidence? That May Be the Reason You're Still Job Searching." Retrieved from http://msn.careerbuilder.com/Article/MSN-2379-Job-Search-Lacking-Confidence-That-May-Be-the-Reason-Youre-Still-Job-Searching/

Dewey, J. (1910). *How We Think*. New York: D. C. Heath.

Enelow, W., and L. Kursmark. (2010). *Cover Letter Magic: Trade Secrets of Professional Resume Writers*, 4th ed. St. Paul, MN: Jist Publishing.

German, K. M., B. E. Gronbeck, D. Ehninger, and A. H. Monroe. (2010). *Principles of Public Speaking*, 17th ed. Boston: Allyn & Bacon.

Grant, A. (2011, January 3). "Want More Clout? Stand Up Straight." *Chicago Tribune*, sec. 6, p. 3.

Hackman, M., and C. Johnson. (2009). *Leadership: A Communication Perspective*, 5th ed. Long Grove, IL: Waveland Press, Inc.

Haefner, R. (2009, October 6). "More Employers Screening Candidates via Social Networking Sites." Retrieved from http://msn.careerbuilder.com/Article/MSN-2035-Job-Info-and-Trends-More-Employers-Screening-Candidates-via-Social-Networking-Sites/

Half, R. (1993, November). "How Do You Prepare for Nonstandard Interviews?" *Management Accounting,* 75(5), 12.

HR World Editors. (2010, August 31). "Thirty Interview Questions You Can't Ask and 30 Sneaky, Legal Alternatives to Get the Same Info." Retrieved from http://www.focus.com/fyi/hr/30-interview-questions-you-cant-ask-and-30-sneaky-legal-get/

Huhman, H. (2009, June 25). "What You Need to Know about Behavioral Interviewing." Retrieved from http://www.examiner.com/x-828-Entry-Level-Careers-Examiner~y2009m6d25-What-you-need-to-know-about-behavioral-interviewing

Ivy, D. K., and P. Backlund. (2004). *GenderSpeak: Personal Effectiveness in Gender Communication*, 3rd ed. New York: McGraw-Hill.

Jacobs, R. (2003). "Communication Skills Self-Assessment Exercise." Retrieved from http://spot.pcc.edu/~rjacobs/career/effective_communication_skills.htm

Jansen, J. (2010). "The 11 Keys to Success." Retrieved from http://jobs.aol.com/articles/2010/04/19/keys-to-success/

Johannesen, R. L., K. S. Valde, and K. E. Whedbee. (2008) *Ethics in Human Communication*. Long Grove, IL: Waveland Press, Inc.

Johnson, S. (2008, January 17). "Reacting to Facebook, Sites Prove We Love to Hate." *Chicago Tribune*, sec. 5, p. 1.

Jolly, D. (2010, August 25). "Germany Plans Limits on Facebook Use in Hiring." Retrieved on August 31, 2010 from http://www.nytimes.com/2010/08/26/business/global/26fbook.html

Kellerman, B. (2008). *Followership: How Followers are Creating Change and Changing Leaders*. Cambridge: Harvard Business School Press.

Kelley, R. (1992). *The Power of Followership: How to Create Leaders that People Want to Follow and Followers Who Lead Themselves*. New York: Doubleday.

Kienzle, N., and S. Husar. (2007). "How Can Cultural Awareness Improve Communication in the Global Workplace?" *Journal of Communication, Speech & Theatre Association of North Dakota*, 20, pp. 81–85.

Kilmann, R. H., and K. W. Thomas. (1977). "Developing a Forced-Choice Measure of Conflict-Handling Behavior: The MODE Instrument." *Educational and Psychological Measurements*, 37, pp. 309–325; see also http://kilmann.com/conflict.html

Kiviat, B. (2009). "Resumé? Check. Nice Suit? Check. Webcam?" *Time*, 174 (18), pp. 49–50.

Krames, J. A. (2008). *Inside Drucker's Brain*. Penguin Books: London.

Krotz, J. (n.d.) "Cell Phone Etiquette: 10 Dos and Don'ts." Retrieved from http://www.microsoft.com/smallbusiness/resources/ArticleReader/website/default.aspx?Print=1&ArticleId=Cellphoneetiquettedosanddonts

Kruger, J., N. Epley, J. Parker, and Z. Ng. (2005). "Egocentrism over E-mail: Can People Communicate as Well as They Think?" *Journal of Personality and Social Psychology*, 89 (6), pp. 925–936.

Ladner, S. (2008). "Laptops in the Living Room: Mobile Technologies and the Divide between Work and Private Time among Interactive Agency Workers." *Canadian Journal of Communication*, 33(3), pp. 465–489.

Littlejohn, S. W., and K. Domenici. (2007). *Communication, Conflict, and the Management of Difference*. Long Grove, IL: Waveland Press, Inc.

Lorenz, K. (2007, September 4). "Ten Attitudes of Successful Workers." Retrieved from http://msn.careerbuilder.com/article/MSN-666-Workplace-Issues-10-Attitude-of-Successful-Workers.com

Lorenz, K. (2009, January 26). "Top 10 Soft Skills for Job Hunters." Retrieved from http://jobs.aol.com/articles/2009/01/26/top-10-soft-skills-for-job-hunters/

Lyons, D. (2011, February). "Ask a Celebrity Geek." *Newsweek*, p. 42.

Madlock, P. (2008). "The Link between Leadership Style, Communicator Competence, and Employee Satisfaction." *Journal of Business Communication*, 45(1), pp. 61–78.

McCracken, H. (2011, February 14). "Query Club." *Time*, 177 (6), p. 53.

McGaan, L. (2003). "Communication: Functions, Perception, Self-concept." Retrieved Oct. 19, 2003, from http://department.monm.edu/cata/McGaan/Classes/cata101/Perception-selfconcept.101.htm

Moody, J., B. Stewart, and C. Bolt-Lee. (2002, March). "Showcasing the Skilled Business Graduate: Expanding the Tool Kit." *Business Communication Quarterly*, 65(1), p. 21.

Muir, C. (2007). "Leadership through Storytelling." *Business Communication Quarterly*, 70(3), pp. 367–369.

Murray, A. (2010, September 21). "What Is the Difference between Management and Leadership?" Adapted from *The Wall Street Journal Guide to Management*. Retrieved from http://guides.wsj.com/management/developing-a-leadership-style/what-is-the-difference-between-management-and-leadership/

Myers, L. L., and R. S. Larson. (2005). "Preparing Students for Early Work Conflicts." *Business Communication Quarterly*, 68(3), pp. 306–317.

Nan, S. A. (2008). "Conflict Resolution in a Network Society." *International Negotiation*, 13(1), pp. 111–131.

OWL. (n.d.). "Writing the Basic Business Letter." Retrieved from http://owl.english.purdue.edu/owl/resource/653/01/

Poundstone, W. (2003). *How Would You Move Mt. Fuji? Microsoft's Cult of the Puzzle—How the World's Smartest Company Selects the Most Creative Thinkers*. New York: Little, Brown.

Ramsey, L. (2004). "Sealing the Deal over the Business Meal." *Consulting to Management—C2M*, 15(4), pp. 22–23.

Reh, J. (n.d.) "Management Skills Pyramid." Retrieved from http://management.about.com/od/managementskills/a/ManagementSkillsPyramid.htm

Ricketts, K. (2009, February). "Competent Leaders: What Effective Leaders Do Well." Retrieved from http://www.ca.uky.edu/agc/pubs/elk1/elk1101/elk1101.pdf

The Right Job. (n.d.) "Objective Writing." Retrieved from http://www.therightjob.com/Resources.aspx?page=1

Roberts, C. (n.d.) "Checklist for Personal Values." Retrieved from http://www.selfcounseling.com/help/personalsuccess/personalvalues.html

Rushmore, S. (2009, June). "The Ultimate Cover Letter." *LodgingHospitality* (LHonline.com), pp. 18–19.

Tahmincioglu, E. (2009, October 16). "Employers Digging Deep on Prospective Workers." Retrieved from http://www.msnbc.msn.com/id/33414017/ns/business-careers/

Tech Directions. (2004, May). "Resumé and Cover Letter Writing Tips." *Tech Directions*, 63 (10), pp. 26–27.

White, D. W., and E. Lean. (2008). "The Impact of Perceived Leader Integrity on Subordinates in a Work Team Environment." *Journal of Business Ethics*, 81, pp. 765–778.

Winter, J. K., J. C. Neal, and K. K. Waner. (2001, September). "How Male, Female, and Mixed-Gender Groups Regard Interaction and Leadership Differences in the Business Communication Course." *Business Communication Quarterly*, 64 (3), pp. 43–58.

Woloshin, M. (2009, February). "Writing Cover Letters—The Perfect Personal Pitch." *Tactics*, p. 7.

Wood, J. (2011). *Gendered Lives: Communication, Gender, and Culture*, 9th ed. Belmont, CA: Cengage.

Wood, J. T. (2004). *Communication Theories in Action: An Introduction*, 3rd ed. Belmont, CA: Wadsworth.

Young, A. M., C. M. Vance, and E. A. Ensher. (2003). "Individual Differences in Sensitivity to Disempowering Acts: A Comparison of Gender and Identity-Based Explanations for Perceived Offensiveness." *Sex Roles: A Journal of Research*, 49 (3/4), pp. 163–171.

Young, K. S., J. T. Wood, G. M. Phillips, and D. J. Pedersen. (2007). *Group Discussion: A Practical Guide to Participation and Leadership*, 4th ed. Long Grove, IL: Waveland Press, Inc.

Zupek, R. (2010, February 24). "Nine Things that Seal the Deal for Hiring Managers." Retrieved from http://www.cnn.com/2010/LIVING/worklife/02/24/cb.seal.job.interview/index.html

Index

231

NOTES

NOTES

NOTES